FOREWORD

Trump clearly meets the definition of a CHUMP: "A stupid or foolish person, a sucker, thinks he is superior and talks constant gibberish". (citations omitted)

His opposition candidates gave all of us clear warnings about his character during the 2016 Presidential election campaign. Here is a sampling:

1. Marco Rubio----Trump is a Con Artist, a most vulgar person, having erratic behavior.
2. Jeb Bush----Trump has no respect for the Constitution, he is a loser, and a chaos candidate.
3. Mitt Romney---- Trump is a Fraud playing Americans for suckers.
4. Ted Cruz---- Trump is a pathological liar, sniveling coward, and a utterly amoral narcissist.
5. Lindsey Graham----Trump is a bigot, equal opportunity abuser, race baiting xenophobic bigot. His rhetoric is Un-American. He is a kook, crazy, and unfit for office. He conned the GOP. He is the world's biggest jackass.

The poems contained herein were composed after the midterms in 2018. They follow the first volume entitled, "Life and times during the reign of President JOKE A. HAUNTUS (From election to the midterms)". That volume covered the first half of Trump's Presidency.

The steady drum beat of his outrageous words and conduct during the second half of his Presidency made most Americans tremble in fear that such a man could be elected for a second term. Many thanks to the wisdom of the US voters who chose to make sure he served only one term. Even as he closed his only term, he predictably was a "Chaos" President. His egotistical behavior led to the hostile "takeover" of the US Capitol building on January 6, 2021. He is the only President ever to be "Impeached" twice. Even so, his bad behavior did not diminish the support from his "Red Hat" base.

I have tried to capture many of the idiotic ways of this man in a humorous but poignant way. Hopefully, these poems will amuse but also cause reflection on what I hope never happens again: the election of a Con Man to the Presidency of the United States.

Many thanks again to my sister, Marian, for her "eye shade sharpie" editing and the patience of my dear wife, Judith Ann. Thanks for the fantastic art work of my grandchildren; Luke, Porter, Walker, Cora, Sol, and Leela-Jean; my daughter Gina; my son Carson and son Clay, creator of the fantastic Trump look-a-like cover; my nephew Joey my brother Al, and sister-in-law Gnelia, AKA Nee-Nee. Enjoy...David Murdach

TROOPS BRACE FOR MARAUDING HORDES

Here they come ready or not!
Those migrant caravan people better not throw rocks.

Trump has ordered us to shoot the rock throwers,
So cock your rifles and wait until they get closer.

Wait a minute! Only one is out there,
But, his cart is full of large bomb-like fare.

Call the bomb squad and get them near,
Yes Sir, right away, "there is real danger here."

Hold your fire! Isn't that Pedro our friendly peddler guy?
You know, the Watermelon Man, whose melons we buy.

Could be, but we can't take the chance,
Those melons may conceal bombs, aiding the
immigrants' advance.

The old Trojan horse trick, eh?
Well it won't work this time, I say.

Alright then, put those melons in your sights,
If we have to shoot "Pedro" we'd better be right.

The marauding immigrant hoards must be close by,
Waiting to see if those melon bombs blow our Trump Wall sky
high.

Maybe they will throw rocks instead,
Even so, Trump says we can shoot them dead.

Kind of perplexing and sad,
Here we are 15,000 troops facing someone's older Dad.

Remember when "Pedro" brought us all gifts?
We all felt bad because he wasn't even on our Christmas list.

Yeah, times have changed for the worse,
Now, we have spreading across our Country an immigrant curse.

We used to wander back and forth across the border,
Now we fly helicopters in search of innocent interlopers.

Why is the Rio Grande now a river of hate?
Can't our Countries ever return to mutual respect before it's too
late?

Well, I for one will be damned,
If I will shoot Pedro, our lovely watermelon man.

Someone has got to say NO!
To the politicians who say "shoot" just for show.

DONALD, PLEASE HELP US

Phone call to Trump Tower Reservation Operator:

Hello, Trump Tower Reservations, how may I help you?
Yes, I'd like to make a reservation for two.

What date(s) would you like sir?
Soon as possible, maybe quicker.

If I may ask, what is the hurry?
Well, my wife and I are in a real flurry.

We've been furloughed from my Government jobs,
Our house is being repossessed like we were robbed.

So we need housing real quick,
I knew who to call for a fix.

Because your owner, Donald Trump, shut the Government down
to our disdain,
He certainly has got to know our pain.

Does that mean you are unemployed now?
Yes, but Trump says we will get paid back somehow.

But sir, you must pay for your stay!
How will you do that without any pay?

I told you, I'm good for the dough,
Just ask Donald, he will know.

OK, I just inquired as you asked,
I just asked Donald and he said go sell something, get some
cash.

Then come back and we can then make a deal,
Who knows, maybe by then the Democrats will kneel.

Donald knows your plight,
And knows you are proud he is having this fight.

No, no, that is not true!
How would you feel if it was you?

Well, don't get touchy,
Consider yourself lucky.

An extended paid vacation,
Is something unheard of for generations.

Just be happy and enjoy the ride,
If pressed, just go Bankrupt as has Donald, with pride!

HELLO, IS ANYONE IN THERE?

The scene: Trump arriving at Capitol for his "Greatest" Speech ever

Here I am at the appointed time,
Where is Congress to hear my words sublime?

I rang the doorbell,
No answer, no one to tell!

Guess Nancy didn't back down,
That bitch just wants to steal my crown.

I'll sneak around to the side and have a peek,
Hope no one thinks I am a peeping tom creep.

Yep, it's just like she said,
All the Congressmen must be in bed.

What a lousy thing for her to do,
Canceling my State of the Union speech with a kick of her shoe.*

Is she afraid of what people will see?
That people might agree with me?

That depriving 800,000 government employees of their earnings,
Is a good thing to get my wall money churning.

I had to keep the Limbaugh, Hannity, Coulter Trinity happy,
Otherwise, they would complain my Presidency is crappy.

So, here I sit on the Capitol steps,
Alone, bewildered but without regrets.

This insubordinate Congress hasn't yet seen me at my best,
I will tell Mitch to destroy the eggs in their nest.

Then the radical left will have to kneel,
Because they'll have no chicks to feed their special interest deals.

My MAGA fans, however, I will keep,
They will follow me without a peep.

They don't have to be taught,
As their brain cells have gone to rot.

---

*House Speaker Nancy Pelosi withdrew her invitation for Trump to give his 2019 State
Of the Union speech until the Government shutdown ended.

TRUMP'S SHUTDOWN SONG

Shut down races have just begun,
Doo Dah, Doo Dah.

If I don't get my Wall after 15 days,
Someone's horse is going to pay.

So, send the immigrants to Guantanamo Bay,
Doo Da, Doo Da Day.

Bet your money on a Democrat nag,
And you'll lose a day's pay.

Shut down races have just begun,
But can't you see I have already won.

Oh, Melania, don't you cry for me,
I came from Mar A Lago with golf clubs on my knee.

Gonna run on fright, Gonna scream all day,
Bet my money on Mitch's Nag, as Dems didn't feed theirs any
hay.

MATADOR TRUMP

Trump's rallies are like bullfights,
Matador Trump performing to the crowd's delight.

Dressed in his dark blue suit and flashy red tie,
He taunts the bullish crowds with his fiendish cries.

The opening speakers are the picadors,
Arousing the crowd by lancing all Democrats across the boards.

He scorches his invisible opponents with his poisonous breath.
His venom becomes his Rejon de Muerte (lance of death).

Casting aside his protective cape,
He prances and dances before the media he calls fake.

And then as his final gasp before his exhausted fans can rest,
He thrusts his verbal dagger into his opponent's chest.

With his kill laying on the stage ever so still,
He struts around puffing out his chest like a large hornbill.

The crowd then ceases to roar,
Knowing their dream has come true as they head for the door.

Being energized until the next rally by their zealot artist,
The bellies of his fans now full after eating on a fresh carcass.

ANOTHER DAY AT THE TRUMP ZOO

Wow! What a mid-term election night!
Trump tried to claim victory despite receiving voters' slight.

He held a press conference, in which he fought with reporters,
Answering their questions with nasty retorts.

He berated CNN's Jim Acosta as being a rude, terrible person,
Telling an aide to take the microphone away like a scalpel from a surgeon.

He blasted fellow Republicans who didn't accept his campaign embrace,
Gloated over the fact that as a result, they lost their race.

Over all it was a sickening display of a self-centered man,
Having no majestic vision for our beautiful land.

His performance contained an animalistic rage,
Lashing, like a carnivorous beast at his keeper from his cage.

TRUMP PLAYS SANCTION MAN

SANCTION MAN huffs and puffs his swollen chest,
Determined to cause Iran unrest.

He starves Iran's people, waiting for their curtsy,
Hoping that its people will fall before him begging for his mercy.

For he rules not with compassion,
Even showing delight in withholding their rations.

His insecurities are demonstrated in his fiscal policies
Claiming the world is giving us a perpetual colonoscopy.

What is he afraid of? Because as he routinely asserts,
Our economy runs every other country into the dirt.

So if Iranian sanctions aren't related to our economic concerns,
Are SANCTION MAN'S actions really because Iran is causing
Israel heartburn?

SANCTION MAN enjoys starving and whipping like a goon,
Similar to slave ships, whipping and starving to get the rowers in
tune.

He won't consider meeting with the leaders of Iran,
Until he has squeezed their necks by his hands.

What he doesn't know is that other countries are proud people,
They know they are being squeezed by a weasel.

He fondly strokes Dictators Kim Jung-un and Putin's hands,
He hopes to cozy up to Iran's Ayatollah Ali Khamenei's clans.

Looking for a photo op meet and greet,
Then kissing the Ayatollah's ring and rubbing his feet.

For our "Greatest President" ever,
Is only interested in expanding his real estate endeavors.

It would be no surprise that he has expansive plans,
To put Trump Towers all over Iran.

---

*After withdrawing the US from the Iran Nuclear deal, Trump re-imposed severe
sanctions on Iran.

GUNFIRE RINGS OUT DURING THE MIDTERM ELECTIONS

OH ME, OH MY!
Why doesn't our country cry?*

We hear the sounds of gunfire once again,
Our ears have grown numb and won't tune in.

All we hear is political noise,
That drowns out gun violence victims' joys.

Moments before the trigger was pulled,
A wonderful human life stood not yet fulfilled.

A simple task it would seem to be,
Investigate and devise a prevention strategy.

What are the underlying causes that bring such pain and grief?
What can be done to give us some relief?

If we can't change or affect an insane person's desire to kill,
It would seem reasonable to take away his/her poisonous pills.

The pills that are being sold come from NRA Pharmacists,
Who dispense without restriction and staunchly persist.

But no, our political leaders can't even speak.
They kneel before the NRA powerless and weak.

We didn't elect the NRA sirens,
We elected leaders to protect our environs.

Lax campaign finance laws don't provide a fix,
Gun happy politicians get huge NRA sums to play their dirty
tricks.

Fat chance the politicians will turn off the money spigot,
But we have to get out of this interminable thicket.

Politics' thorny intertwined brambles and vines,
Are frustrating to our citizens' reasonable minds.

We must cut through these sticky political bushes,
Clearing a path to solving potential killers' wishes.

---

*On November 7, 2018, the day after the midterm elections, 13 people were killed in a
mass shooting in California.

McRAVEN, YOU ARE A LOSER!

Trump Speaks:

I could have caught Osama Bin Laden much sooner,
I knew where he was, it was obvious even to losers.

Of course, Admiral McRaven is a critic of mine,
But putting that aside, I could have killed Bin Laden in no time.*

My motive is not to get back at McRaven because he doesn't like me,
I stated in my 2000 book that Bin Laden was a threat to our country.

If only our leaders would read my books,
They would learn how the world works.

I am president and available twenty four seven,
So, come all and sit before me, including you, Admiral McRaven.

My wonderfulness wasn't recognized for years,
Now the world is learning, but not before unnecessary tears.

People, even McRaven, now realize I should be consulted,
On everything, before I act impulsive.

So everyone in the chain of command,
Check my tweets and you will see what the world now understands.

---

*In November 2018, Trump criticized Admiral McRaven for not killing Osama Bin Laden earlier. He, Trump, said he noted the danger of Bin Laden in his 2000 book.

DANCE TRUMP AWAY

We are swinging in the pain,
Cringing at the thought of Trump getting re-elected again.

So grab your partner and saunter to the left,
Don't Dosey Doe with any right wing nut pest.

Form circles around the room,
Sweep away sadness by singing sweet tunes.

Hippity, hoppity, jump up and down,
It will make you forget Trump's evil frown.

Flush from your thoughts his lethal force order,
To shoot immigrants trying to cross our southern border. *

Keep dancing and twirling until you're ready to drop,
Open your eyes and poof! The Trump bad dream will abruptly
stop.

You see, Trump is really a figment of our imagination,
How could this fiend in reality stain our great nation?

So, keep on spinning and dancing after your energy surge,
We don't want a president like Trump to ever re-emerge.

---

*In November 2018, Trump authorized lethal force, if necessary, against immigrants in a
caravan that had reached our southern border.

TRUMP ANSWERS MUELLER'S INTERROGATORIES

Mueller has given Trump some homework to do,
Sending him written questions about his Russian collusion do-
do.

Trump has been dragging his feet about turning them in,
Suspiciously, he says his answers are from his own pen.

He says the answers were easy and he did them in a flash,
Claiming he didn't ask his lawyers to do his task.

His scribbled answers under the light of the midnight oil,
Would probably make his English teachers recoil.

His struggles with truth in words from his lips,
Will be even more noticeable when reading his gobbledygook
penmanship.

He signs his name with such dramatic flare,
Would he be so bold when playing Truth-or-Dare.

He will attempt to obfuscate and evade,
Turning this whole exercise into a game of charades.

RIDICULOUS BEYOND RIDICULOUSNESS

Trump won't listen to the Khashoggi murder tape,*
Claiming he won't learn anything new about his fate.

Also refusing to listen is National Security Advisor Bolton,
His excuse that it is in Arabic is revolting.

What if it was a recording of Hitler?
Saying he can't understand German would be a side splitter.

What if it was a recording of Putin?
Saying he can't understand Russian would lead to loud hooting.

These alleged leaders are eating their own crow,
Refusing to exercise their duties is a sad sideshow.

They loved to listen to Wiki-leaks tapes,
But with Saudi Arabia they are afraid of who the tapes may
implicate.

Trump says, "Crown Prince Salman is a great man,
He may or may not have participated in the murder plan."

"So what if the CIA says to the contrary,
This is a story that I will bury."

"The only problem that I might not be able to untangle,
Is if parts of Khashoggi's body are on Crown Prince Salman's
mantle."

---

*In November 2018, Trump and National Security Advisor Bolton refused to listen to the Khashoggi murder tape.

LIES AND MORE LIES

Hickory dickory dock,
I hope I can run out the clock.

Mueller is closing in,
On my covert business with Putin.

So what if I was negotiating a hotel deal during the campaign,*
It didn't go through so what is there to disdain.

Perfectly OK for me to wheel and deal,
So what if I lied about my efforts to make my dream real.

You see I always wanted to build a Trump Tower,
In Red Square as a backdrop to Russia's military power.

While Russia' military might is on display,
My Tower would shimmer during their extravagant parade.

With my tall image in the background,
The world would watch spellbound.

America is great don't get me wrong,
But as I continually say, "why, we and Russia can't get along."

I have not committed any sin,
Unabashed Capitalism is the business I am in.

I am still sorry my Moscow Tower wasn't a go,
It would have been another star in my massive ego.

No harm, no foul I say,
I didn't build it. So, Mueller stay away.

Put your arrow back in your quiver,
Point your bow at those Democratic slickers.

You see, money for me is like winning a race,
Being President only comes in second place.

---

*In late November 2018, Michael Cohen, Trump's former personal Attorney, admitted he lied when he previously claimed before Congress that Trump's efforts to negotiate with Russia to build a Trump Tower didn't spill over into Trump's Presidential campaign.

POOR DONALD

Eeny, meeny miny mo,
Where did my friends at the G-20 go?

I looked all around for any smiling face,
But all I got in return were looks of disgrace.

I shaved and deodorized quite heavily,
I didn't stink so my friends should have been in ecstasy.

But instead they greeted me with a frown,
Compared to Obama whom they thought was wearing a crown.

Is it because they can't stand my beautiful sight?
They are probably just jealous of my intellectual might.

At any rate I feel a little sad and lonely,
Seeing my friends not eating up my baloney.

I want to be the center of attention to the world kingdom,
While all the world leaders sit before me soaking up my profound
wisdom.

Crown Prince Salman and Putin created quite a spectacle,
Their greeting resembled them grasping each other's testicles.*

I would have enjoyed that kind of attention,
Instead I just sit alone in my room admiring my mirror's
reflection.

---

*At the G-20 Brazilian Summit held in December, 2018, Trump appeared to be lost in the crowd. Putin and Crown Prince Salaman gave each other an over the top vigorous handshake that went viral on the Internet.

TRUMP, THE TARIFF MAN

There is a new Tariff Man in town,
He walks with a swagger his smiles are like a frown.

He is tall, bleached blonde and portly,
Some say he will be out of office shortly.

But for now he trolls the trade routes,
Looking for unfair trade deals to squeeze like grapefruit.

He thinks the US is getting the short end on trade,
So he has made this issue a daily crusade.

He clomps down the trade lanes,
His sharp stirrups ready to inflict economic pain.

Thinking the US is always the loser makes him feel pain,
Getting the short end of any deal is not in his brain.

If he discovers he has not completely prevailed in negotiations,
He will nonetheless spin it in his direction.

No matter if he has failed, it is always a win,
To Tariff Man losing is a sin.

---

* After his dinner at the G-20 Summit in December 2018, with Chinese President Xi,
Trump said, "I am Tariff Man".

TRACKING TRUMP

Greetings from Ye Old professional Presidential foot trackers,
We follow the tracks of American Presidents, looking for
slackers.

In the past, Presidential footprints go in a straight line,
Or, maybe straying to the left or right some of the time.

But Trump's tracks don't stay the course,
They veer and swerve like a wounded horse.

Normally, Presidential tracks reflect honesty in the effort,
Showing the smooth gait of a strong Shepherd.

But Trump's are wobbly tracks,
Evidence that he is making up his own facts.

Of major concern is his prints' pivoting spin,
Displaying a propensity to lie to save his skin.

His gait is lumbering and halting during times of stewing,
Showing his days have long periods of TV viewing.

Wow, look at this, there are high heel prints, could be whose?
Holy smokes, now his prints are in between those spike shoes.

Looks like Stormy may have again caught her prey,
These revolting tracks hopefully will soon melt away.

THE WOLF IS IN THE HEN HOUSE

What the Hell! He fired Jeff Sessions,
Won't this pig-headed President ever learn his lesson.

Sure looks like he wants to end the Mueller probe,
Just like an antibiotic does to a microbe.

With daily doses of "no collusion" injections,
He hopes to stay in office until the next election.

He now has appointed Sessions' replacement,
Matthew Whitaker, whose office was in the basement.

Acting and panicking in fear,
It appears his plan to halt Mueller is perfectly clear.

He's a cornered rat waiting for the trap to snap,
Bristling and squirming like there is a hot pepper under his hat.

Whitaker, as the new Acting Attorney General will have to change his spots,
Previously he has criticized the Mueller/Russia probe a lot.

Now, the hen house is open for Wolf Whitaker to prowl,
While he, Trump, fiendishly watches and listens for the grisly growls.

CORNERED

Here I sit on top of my golden mushroom stool,
Circled by my administration's ship of fools.

Loyalty is a thing of the past,
My fixer Attorney sicked Mueller on my ass.

Cohen turned into a "RAT",
Bringing me problems to combat.

If that wasn't enough to fight,
Now comes my friend Pecker and ladies of the night.

They are bringing my philandering ways to roost,
Threatening to reveal my unseemly juice.

Pecker knows of my efforts to kill the stories,
Concerning my braggadocious sexual glories.

My money payments to prostitutes were not illegal,
I tried to hide them using Cohen, my legal Beagle?

With Pecker and Cohen in the public's ears,
I will divert attention to my favorite immigration fears.

I will use same playbook again and again,
Changing the subject to Americans being affected by immigrants'
stain.

TWINS

Trump and McConnell are joined at the hip,
Confident they will force the Democrats to eat their own shit.

To hell with public shame,
Ego is their game.

It is really not about the wall,
That isn't it at all.

These two clowns,
Have smiles that are actually frowns.

They are simply playing chicken,
Trying to avoid an election licking.

They don't care about immigrant hordes,
They just want an election issue score.

What a pair they be,
One with thinning fake golden hair, the other, eyes like beads.

They strut their manhood behind microphone veils,
Speaking words like sharpened nails.

For shut down workers no sympathy or sorrow,
Just words from their hacks they borrow.

Why should the Country have to suffer while these two souls,
Cheerfully play in their slimy political mud holes.

They need a time out to gather their juvenile thoughts,
To re-learn how "wall" legislation should be brought.

Not by either Presidential slippery,
Or, by Senate trickery.

But by the "will" of the people,
Who, for now, sit quietly in the shadow of legislative steeples.

Both twins are unhinged,
They want a wall like Stonehenge.

That encircles the whole US with large-type boulders,
With portals of GOP saints spaced around its shoulders.

In the center there will be a combat zone,
Featuring ICE WARRIORS against UNARMED immigrants who
are alone.

Only by surviving this unfair test,
Will they grant entrance into the US.

PERFECT ME

I am the Champion,
My ego is larger than all my mansions.

Can't everybody see,
What a perfect specimen I be.

My rhymes and nicknames cause piercing wounds,
Making my antagonists look like buffoons.

I say, "Build a Wall,
And Crime will Fall."

Those clever words in verse,
Will be my "Wall" opponents' worst curse.

No one can out-rhyme me,
Just anyone try and see.

What, a new challenger in the ring?
Calling himself the "Doggerel King".

Give me your best shot, "slimeball",
What's the matter, too small to crawl?

"Not at all", Doggerel King replies,
"It is hard to see past the hate in your eyes."

"Your rhymes are goofy and hollow,
Mine are like arrows from Apollo."

"You use your ignorant words,
Entertaining your flock of nerds."

My razor sharp thoughts,
Enlighten and can't be bought.

"By the way, your wall rhyme would be better this way, "Protect my mighty wall, for I am so small".

BIG POD, NOT MUCH INSIDE

Trump's body shell is large,
Inside, however, there is only a small garage.

Housing a mind the size of two peas,
Common sense floats in a bucket of sleaze.

There is a workbench with some of his favorite tools,
Designed to only be used by fools.

They show considerable wear and tear,
To be expected as he tweets incessantly on the air.

Some of these tools have familiar names,
Hatred, bigotry, and slander are a few that have earned him fame.

He appears to be working on a "wall",
Looks like, however, it is quite small.

It is in the election issue "illegal immigrant" bin,
Next to the drawer labeled "gifts for Putin".

This small wall looks as if it was to be a room divider with a mirror,
But then changed to be outside as the election draws near.

There are older "Vote Democratic" signs in storage,
From the days he parked his political ship in Democrat moorage.

Now he has "GOP" plastered all over the place,
Surrounding a dartboard shaped like HILLARY'S face.

There is no reading material,
Replaced by a giant keyboard, making it all more surreal.

Looking out his eyes is a real psychedelic trip,
Through his lenses you see greed rising from a dark crypt.

There are lists of romantic adventures that he has sown,
Posted right above his twitter phone.

All in all, it is a depressing sight,
With no sign of compassion to do what is right.

JUST LIKE IN ALICE IN WONDERLAND

He's painting the roses red,
He's painting the roses red.

Criticism about immigrant beds,
He's painting that black rose red.

Wrong about El Paso being a crime bed,
He's painting that black rose red.

Rebuffed about a wall and told "better security" instead,
He's painting that black rose red.

Criticized over the Obama Iran Nuclear Deal shred,
He's painting that black rose red.

Critics say Emergency Wall Declaration has misled,
He's painting that black rose red.

Changing colors of the subject is his favorite trick,
He thinks "clever", but we say "sick".

He flips a negative upside down,
Loudly lying with the voice of a clown.

But, sadly "his people" enjoy the show from the safety of their beds,
While he, like the Queen of Hearts paints the roses red.

Trumpty Dumpty
took a great fall . . .

by: Gnelia

THAT'S OUR GUY

Walking down the street,
Big Donald can be heard going tweet, tweet.

With each stumbling stride,
He attacks anyone he chooses with pride.

He doesn't hold back,
On his slanderous attacks.

He mouths fusillades of snarls from his hateful trunk,
Continuously reloading with bursts of distasteful gunk.

"That's our President", we say to others with chagrin,
It's hard to excuse a man who wallows in a bathtub of sin.

DICTATOR TRUMP

Striking his Mussolini-like pose,
He pirouettes to display his silhouette's pronounced nose.

His crowd doesn't catch on,
They are in awe and continue to fawn.

Socialism seems to be on his mind,
But yet he wants to his fans to follow him blind.

Like a Dictator he wants to run the news,
Giving only his version to his constituents who sit adoringly in their pews.

Any kind of criticism he labels as fake,
Hoping to change the issue that is in debate.

Sure sounds like he is a Socialist Dictator in disguise,
Controlling the Country through his angry eyes.

THERE HE GOES AGAIN

You, Mr. Trump, claim not raking the brush,
Contributed to the California devastating fire rush.

If so, why don't you put the caravan of migrants to work,
Give them shovels and pitch forks.

Send them in with equipment in hand,
To go forth and save our forestlands.

Their young children could sweep dry brush away,
If they want asylum make them work rather than play.

Even as the fires roar, you continue to deny climate change is a factor,
Keeping your head in the sand along with corporate benefactors.

You trotted through the fire scene debris,
Like you were walking to the 9th tee.

You made insignificant comments while pointing to rubble,
Where family homes stood, now are hovels.

You claim Finland rakes its forests and has no problems,
But the Finnish President says that claim is made up by goblins.

If you are serious to do so here, your words for the new hats that you've chosen,
Should be "Make America Rake again" as your new slogan.

TRUMP SPEAKS ABOUT HIS "LOVE" FOR KIM
AT VIET NAM SUMMIT

We are in love,
Kim and I are like two Turtle Doves.

Sitting on a branch cooing in the wind,
Wrapping our wings around each other like twins.

We happily tweet together our loving melody,
We have put aside our past indiscretions in our mutual ecstasy.

You say Kim has a murderous past?
What man hasn't strayed from his path?

You say I have been in the past adulterous and dishonest,
"So what", says Kim, we have wonderful mutual fondness.

Nothing can break our loving bonds,
Not even a Teensy-Weensy nuclear bomb.

As long as my new pal Kim doesn't test it, I'm fine,
After all he, like me, has to make sure his enemies don't cross
the line.

I understand he has North Korea to protect,
His weapons will be handy to guard the buildings I will erect.

Kim is teaching me how to build a great wall,
He has one, concrete, land mines, barbed wire and all.

We both agree that to keep our countries safe from illegal entry,
Big, bad, and deadly barriers act as an effective sentry.

The more I talk to Kim, I find we have much in common,
The fruits of our love for each other will continue to blossom.

Because I am so wonderful with Dictators, my critics fulminate,
I would have "loved" Hitler in Munich in '38.

WHAT CAN WE BELIEVE?

What happened to the idea of a candidate having a platform,
Now it is simply an insulting firestorm.

No grand ideas are discussed,
Instead, we get a showman's clever disgust.

Laughter and smirks carry the day,
While serious issues are kept at bay.

TV personalities have a leg up,
Giving them a head start to gain voters' trust.

Today Mr. Trump, self proclaimed TV star, exclaimed,
"The charges against me are bullshit", suggesting he is being
framed.*

Never in my short life have I heard a President speak this way,
Seems like the oven door is open and he is feeling the heat
coming his way.

This follows his continuing love fest with Kim Jong-un of North
Korea,
Taking his word about Otto Warmbier amounted to verbal
diarrhea.

 A short time ago Trump was excoriating Kim for mistreating Otto,
Now he believes Kim's statement that he didn't know of his woe.

What can we believe from this man's lips,
When he weaves nonsense into a quilt of "bullshit".

---

*On March 2, 2019, speaking before the conservative CPAC group he claimed the
accusations against him by the special counsel were "bullshit". On the last day of his
Viet Nam summit with Kim Jong-un he proclaimed he took his word that he knew nothing
of Otto Warmbier's medical condition before being released from prison in North Korea
and returned to the US where he soon died. Mr. Warmbier was a student. He was
imprisoned for stealing a political poster. The Warmbier family attended Trump's State of
the Union speech in which he vigorously criticized North Korea and its leadership.

YO HO HO

The submarine USS Trump sails in the sea of hate,
With its Captain, Joke A. Hauntus, and his twin, McConnell, as
first mate.

"Up Periscope", cries Captain Joke, "I'm looking off our prow,
I see Destroyer Cohen bearing down on us now."

"Quickly load the Torpedo tubes with explosive scandal,
We need red meat that will be too hot for him to handle."

"Let's see, we have used "no collusion" and "witch hunt",
What would knock out this ratty runt?"

"Our dogged portrayal of his lying past has damaged his ship,
But we need to sink him with a splash of disgust like good old
sheep dip."

"His ship is a parasite approaching our rear,
We need to stop him before he gets near."

"So, fire those Torpedoes at his ship,
Make him no more than a radar blip."

"What, our bombs were off target?
Load them up, fire again, hit him in the gut."

"Captain, it looks like his ship is still coming close,
Our latest bombs were just near him at most."

"The only explosive we have left,
Is the "Bullshit" bomb you've held close to your vest."

"Dumbos! Fire it and don't miss,
If Bullshit doesn't work, I'll really be pissed."

DON'T WORRY, NO INCOME NO PROBLEM
(GOVERNMENT SHUTDOWN 2019)

Wilbur Ross, Commerce Secretary, said get a loan,
Or take out a mortgage on your home.

This was his message to Government employees out of work,
The shut down is necessary to wall off immigrant crooks.*

Your sacrifice of living without wages,
Will be recognized as honorable for the ages.

You ask about Daycare and Medical expenses,
Not my problem, what we really need is bigger immigrant fences.

I say to you furloughed workers, "stay strong,"
The cost to you is minor compared to ringing victory's gong.

Worse comes to worst, bankruptcy is available,
Not for me, of course, because I am not replaceable.

So carry on and don't be glum,
Your Great Golden Domed leader won't let you become a bum.

I will blow the whistle when it is time to go back to work,
In the meantime, maybe get a job as a soda jerk.

---

*In early 2019, the Federal Government had the longest partial shutdown in history over
President Trump demanding money for his Wall on the US Mexico border. As a result,
the affected Federal employees received no pay while the Government was shut down.

WHAT ME WORRY? JUST POLITICAL PROBES

Holy Smoke, this is nothing but Presidential harassment,
81 requests for documents is a political embarrassment. *

I will, of course, comply as it's my Presidential duty,
However, only to requests I don't consider snooty.

I am above reproach,
Slightly above Jesus and the Holy Ghost.

"No Collusion" is my refrain,
I say it over and over again.

Repetition is my style,
I say it many times with a smile.

Sooner or later I believe it myself,
Then I begin undulating and roaring like a magical elf.

I then cast a spell over my swaying fans,
Making them like zombies following my plans.

They march out of the arena under my control.
Staying undercover like blinded moles.

When I beckon for their attention,
They will rise up and salute without dissension.

For they recognize what the Democrats don't,
The GOP is in my castle surrounded by an impenetrable moat.

---

* Following the midterm elections the new Democratic controlled House of
Representatives issued 81 subpoenas for information on the Trump Empire and it's
activities.

OUR EXTINCTION?
(Lesson from the Dinosaurs)

A long, long time ago a large egg opened to a vulture chorus,
Giving birth to a new Dinosaur species, Trumpanalsaurus.

It could have been called an Oviraptor beast,
Known as a voracious egg thief.

Or a Carnotaurus, whose stomach was never full,
Having a reputation of being a meat-eating bull.

Both names could apply,
But he was really, really an unusual guy.

The name "Trump" stands for a weak-kneed, sloth-type jerk,
Who always gives everyone a silly smirk.

The word "anal" needs no explanation,
For his mind was always whirling in sexual exploitation.

So combined, "Trumpanalsaurus" was a perfect name,
To describe a new species some consider insane.

He was a fat little thing with a blonde quiff up top,
Not very stable on his legs, causing a serious rock.

He wobbled along to and fro,
Trying hard to balance on his little toes.

In his childhood he took advantage of his Dinosaur mates,
Piggishly eating with no hesitation from their plates.

Most of his friends had large paws to help them clutch,
But Trumpanalsaurus had tiny fingers that didn›t help much.

He had Lizard like hips,
And blood thirsty lips.

He mostly sat alone in his own world of pretend,
Thinking of nicknames for each of his so-called friends.

He really didn't have close ties,
He ended any chances of friendship with words of despise.

Why did he act this way?
His mother and father couldn't say.

Whatever the reason, he never changed,
Issuing epithets of hate like a mind deranged.

He was spoiled, never having to hunt for his food,
His mother and father abundantly fed him and their brood.

His parents marveled at their new wonder child,
Sitting in awe of his quick-witted style.

As he grew older he really became a big family pain,
Always claiming to others he was on top of his game.

The other Dinosaurs began to rebel,
Finally telling him loudly, GO TO HELL!

So, dragging his tail he left the family nest,
Venturing out on his worldly quest.

During his adventure he met some real slime balls,
First, he met Manafort, the Muskox, who later lived in a prison stall.

Then he saddled up with Wombat Wissenberg,
Who became his accounting nerd.

Then be befriended Possum Pecker, a master handler,
Protecting Trumpanalsaurus against accusations of being a philanderer.

So their journey led them down corruption road,
By cheating, stealing, and lying in criminal mode.

While on their way,
They devoured many a prey.

Not caring who or what they encountered,
Destroying their opponents even when surrounded.

Then one day, Trumpanalsaurus decided to be in supreme command,
Of all of the creatures in Dinosaur land.

He mocked his plant-eater opponents,
Calling them veggie rodents.

He degraded his fellow meat eaters,
By suggesting they were cheaters.

He refused to release his own personal information,
Joking his critics drank too much libation.

This method of dealing with his enemies,
Wherein he sarcastically pivoted, became one of his specialties.

Sadly, the Dinosaur world bought into his ugly campaign,
Anointing him the leader of all their terrain.

Some say as a result of that election,
It caused the Dinosaur extinction.

Does our orange-headed leader share the same DNA,
With the evil Trumpanalsaurus, that didn>t let anything stand in
his way?

Is our current Trump related to Trumpanalsaurus?
If so, what stands before us?

It is an ugly thought to ponder,
But history should cause us to wonder.

Our President has lizard like hips,
Meaty McDonald's Hamburger juice drips from his lips.

His hateful behavior is the same,
Trumpanalsaurus did as much in his political game.

As for the "anal" part of the Trumpanalsaurus sociopath,
Our President is really a big pain in the Ass.

Donald Trump, therefore, is definitely in
the Trumpanalsaurus family tree,
With that fact in mind, how worried should we be?

To stop our extinction, a la Dinosaurs, by this grisly beast,
We need to immediately impeach him and have a great feast.

Then all mankind can look at each other,
Recognizing we are not enemies but a world of brothers.

"Trumpanalsaurus"
by: Porter

TRUMP: WHAT ME A WHITE NATIONALIST?

My outstanding fair statements:

"I think there is blame on both sides. You had some bad people in that group (white nationalists) but you also had people that were very fine people on both sides"*

* (2017, Charlottesville, Virginia, March by white nationalists where one person was killed and hundreds of white persons marching chanting, «you can›t replace us», against Jews and non-whites)

"White Nationalism is not a rising threat around the world. I think it is a small group of people that have very, very serious problems". *

*(2019, Christchurch, NZ, 50 people mass murdered by a white nationalist who said Trump was a symbol of renewed white identity)

Fake news is obsessed with my great speeches,
But they act like a bunch of blood-sucking leeches.

They suck the truth from my words,
Printing a bias against my powerful nouns and verbs.

When I say White Nationalists are friends of mine,
I am not saying they are right all the time.

I am merely pointing out that they have a right,
To talk about a White person's plight.

Sure there are bad apples in their mix,
But I am sure it is a small number who play dirty tricks.

Wouldn't you agree that our nation would be brought to its knees,
If it wasn't for real White people rather than their wannabes?

GREAT NEWS!

When Trump received the news that Mueller found "No Collusion",
He trumpeted those words to stifle any confusion.

Unabashedly and without reserve,
He gloated without fearing striking anyone's nerves.

He puffed and bellowed to a large degree,
Snorting his innocence for everyone to see.

With his mouth pursed and drawing his lips tight,
He shouted, "Mueller found No Collusion, proving me right."

His mouth resembled a Sphincter muscle experiencing a moment,
Opening to discharge sewage words about his opponents.

He curiously said no President should be under an investigator's grip,
Forgetting he spuriously investigated Obama's citizenship.

I TOLD YOU SO!

I am beside myself with the great news,
Mueller has agreed with my well-reasoned views.

I told you there was no collusion*,
That it was an issue created by Democrat illusions.

Now, as for "Obstruction of Justice", that is also a joke,
That was an issue created by the same Democrat folks.

Can't he see my conduct is beyond reproach,
I am untouchable in my gilded coach.

My fans wave and clamor to get me in selfie views,
They adore me while putting aside any negative reviews.

I may have said Mueller was a bad dude,
And that his probe was a witch hunt, silly and crude.

But now that he has fully exonerated me,
Mueller is an honorable man and my comments were really just
a tease.

My fans understand as a part of my humor I frequently mock,
Just like when I said, "as a star I can grab women by the pussy",
was locker room talk.

---

*After an extensive investigation, Special Prosecutor Robert Mueller sent a report to Attorney General Barr who in turn summarized it stating that there was not sufficient evidence that Donald Trump coordinated or conspired with Russians to influence the outcome of the 2016 Presidential election. Importantly, Mueller also wrote that there was not sufficient evidence to exonerate him from a charge of Obstruction of Justice.

WHOOPEE I AM FREE!

Hey, Hey, here you go,
Mueller exonerated me don't you know.*

Read his report, no collusion, no obstruction you can see,
He concluded I am totally off Scot free.

Whew, it was close but I finally prevailed,
But those scummy Democrats are still on my trail.

So what if I answered Mueller's written questions "I couldn't recall",
Yes, I have stated on several occasions I have the greatest memory of all.

But that doesn't mean Mueller's questions were fair game,
After all, my Lawyers didn't want me to play his game.

So I hedged my bets and claimed no recollection,
When actually I do recall, I'll keep that a secret for my own protection.

Time now to switch gears,
I will dump illegal immigrants in Sanctuary cities to see their fears.*

So when the fake news concentrates on that,
I will get my corrupt agenda back on track.

---

* On April 18, 2019, Robert Mueller›s released his report concerning the Russian interference in the 2016 Presidential election.

* On April 12, 2019, Trump announced he is considering placing illegal immigrants in Sanctuary Cities.

SORRY, THERE IS NO ROOM FOR YOU

Sorry, we are full, *
Turn around, immigrants, no room, not even for a handful.

Well maybe not for some Norwegians and blonde Swedes,
But brown people, this Country doesn't need.

So close the screen door at the border,
Those poor immigrants are like flies trying to create disorder.

You ask, what about affluent countries?
They will still be welcome with unlimited bounties.

There are enough illegals in this country for me to hire,
To service my golf courses to meet my desire.

I don't need any more, so go back to your human strife,
Who cares if there is threat of rape for your wife.

Just stay on the other side of my giant slated fence,
You can look through but don't get the idea of digging a trench.

It is just the way it is, so just get used to it,
It may a long wait so be prepared to sit.

---

*President Trump has announced that this country is filled to capacity of immigrants,
"We are full", he stated.

PEOPLE WHO LIVE IN GLASS HOUSES

Trump at poolside: Are you the new towel boy?
You look brown-skinned, are you legal to be in my employ?

If not, we will have to cut a deal,
So, I won't squeal.

I will pay you under the table so keep quiet,
If word got out, it could cause a fake news riot.

Of course, we'll have to cut a deal on your pay,
Probably trimming the minimum wage by half, wouldn't you say?

Towel Boy replies:
What do you think I am, you saggy jowl-faced orange bastard?,
A Slave, of which you have many, in your vast herd?

Trump replies:
Whoa, you pint-sized illegal,
Do as I say or I will pen a name for you, like dung beetle.

Now, notify the chef we are adding a table at dinner,
I have invited all my past cabinet sinners.

Steve Bannon is among them, as my special guest,
Who is a wonderful guy, a standout, in my corruption nest.

You'll learn my dear illegal friend,
You need crooks on whom you can always depend.

MY HEALTHCARE PLAN IS GREAT

Come, all my fans, sit on my knee,
Gather around to hear my health care plan for thee.*

No worry about seeing my plan,
Because all I have to do is tweak my nose and say "Shazam"!

It will be a great plan that will gain your trust,
Not some Obama ideas made of fairy dust.

We will have great heath care, just you wait,
You ask for the details, sorry, I won't take the bait.

The plan is in my great golden head,
Soon to be printed, distributed and read.

So just you wait and see,
My plan will shake up the heath industry.

To do that, of course, will require all of you,
To sacrifice the benefits you may think are due.

Pre-existing conditions protection has to go,
Too costly my statistics show.

Staying on your parents plan until twenty-six,
Nah, those spoiled kids can find their own fix.

Healthcare Exchanges to help the poor and not the wealthy,
Nope, that 's gone for they need to do as I do, eat healthy.

We're going to go back to the good old times,
Where the rich get care, the poor only in jail after committing
crimes.

---

*Trump, to the surprise everyone, including members of the Republican Party, soon after the release of the Mueller Report announced that the Republican Party would now be known as the Party of Health Care. The Republicans didn't have an alternative plan to Obama Care at the time of this announcement. They still don't.

TRUMP'S MESSAGE TO IRAN

Don't tread on the US, Iran,
If you do I'll turn you into quicksand.

I am the huffy puffy US dragon master,
My head is the tangerine-looking twitter broadcaster.

No one beats me at my game,
Those who have tried have ended up lame.

My forked tongue tells many tales,
All are lies but my supporters don't sweat the details.

Anyway, I digress, I don't want War,
But putting the world under stress is something I adore.

CUCKOO, COUP KOO

Now Trump has really gone Cuckoo,
Claiming he was the victim of an attempted coup.*

Doubtful he really knows what he is saying,
Everyday his blather is becoming more dismaying.

He claims the wrong horse won the Kentucky Derby,
Shows he is spending too much time playing with his Barbies.

To top it all, later he spent an hour or so on the phone with Putin,
He's not telling what they talked about, but it sure wasn't about
avoiding gluten.

He claimed Putin smiled when the Mueller probe was mentioned,
How he knew this from the phone explains his mental
suspension.

For bloviated Donald continues to leak wordy gas,
Mumbling and grumbling about the Mueller report morass.

He must be a fit to behold at home behind the curtain,
Knowing that his full term as President is all but uncertain.*

---

*As of May 16, 2019, the talk of impeachment was growing louder due to Trump's
directives to disallow the House subcommittee to receive the un-redacted Mueller
Report and its underlying documentation.

HA HA

Na, Na, Na, can't catch me,
Your subpoenas are a pile of dust below my knees.

I am king of the government. I have the upper hand,
Your subpoenas will not stand.

Just like Hickory Dickory Dock,
I am the louse that is going to run out the clock.

I will appeal, appeal, appeal,
You will hear my legal team's wheels squeal.

I have the legal system figured out,
My strategy will cause you grief, leaving you only to pout.

WIND BAG

The bigoted golden bloviator-in-chief has done it again,
Claiming to be a "stable genius" while speaking like a clucking
hen.*

A cluck, cluck here, and a cluck, cluck there,
He manages to keep clucking without moving a hair.

His clucks are getting repetitious and just plain dumb,
One wonders if he composes them while sitting on his thumb.

He just clucked that he agrees with Kim Jong-un,
That Joe Biden is a low IQ goon.*

This cluck came on his visit to Japan,
While with Prime Minister Abe, whom he considers his man.

Prior to this meeting, he clucked that House Speaker Pelosi is a
"mess",*
Something she said must have put him in distress.

After he abruptly left their meeting on infrastructure,
She did call for an intervention due to his bizarre departure.*

Then the inexplicable, he left Bolton and Abe chewing gristle,
By saying "no problem" with North Korea firing off short
range missiles.*

Bolton and Abe said by doing so, North Korea violated a UN
resolution,*
But he clucked that it wouldn't cause his friendship with
Kim Jong-un to loosen.

Clearly, the world despots have our President's ear,
Putin, Prince Salman, and Kim Jong-un each are held dear.*

While our faithful friendly countries are sent to the back of the
bus,
Our bloated Clucker is wildly driving us like a muckenfuss.*

*In May 2019, Senator minority leader Chuck Schumer and Speaker of he House Nancy Pelosi met with President Trump to discuss legislation on infrastructure. Trump abruptly left the meeting claiming he couldn't work with the Democrats as long as they were investigating him. Ms. Pelosi before the meeting had stated Trump was involved in a cover up. After the short meeting, Ms. Pelosi called on Trump's family and friends to do an intervention. For his retort, Trump claimed, Ms. Pelosi is a mess and she isn't the same, as he had been watching her for sometime. Referencing the claim that he was somehow mentally unfit he said he is a "stable genius". He publicly called on his cabinet members to verify how calm he was after he left the Pelosi/Schumer meeting.

* During Trump's May 2019 visit to Japan he said he had no problems with North Korea firing off short-range missiles. This position is contrary to what his National Security Advisor John Bolton and Prime Minister Abe had said to the effect that such firings were in violation of the UN resolution covering this subject.

*Muckenfuss---A backwoods toothless redneck found in the outskirts of the Carolinas.

Urban Dictionary

TALE OF TALES

Deep in the D.C. swamp far from here to there,
Sits little fuzzy A.G. Barr Wabbit in his lair.

He's called Barr Wabbit for short,
As he always looks like he is going to snort.

Some say he is lonely in his quiet place,
Spending his days planning his big escape.

Suddenly one day his wish came to pass,
The Golden Mar-a-Lago Ferret gave him a specific task.

The Golden One's Aura did the speaking,
Telling him never to reveal their conversation by leaking.

In whispered tones Craggy Goldie repeatedly asked,
"Barr Wabbit", are you up for this task?

"I want you to read this Mueller report and slant its views,
Make me look like a cherub in a church pew."

"But how can I sincerely say words that I despise",
Sniffled Barr Wabbit, with fake tears running from his eyes.

"Don't worry, I do it all the time with no regrets,"
Grumbled the irritated large-headed Golden Ferret.

"Now remember, cast me in a good light,
You'll be rewarded in golden carrots sweeter than Turkish delights."

So, that's when Barr Wabbit began his formidable task,
Turning a negative Mueller report into a false hero mask.

What he produced was a sight to behold,
Painting the Golden Ferret as being sincere and bold.

"I told you so," screeched the huffy Golden Ferret,
No Collusion, no obstruction, so there, fake news, grin and bear it.

Mueller became upset at Barr Wabbit for manicuring his report,
The Democrats demanded he testify or they would see him in court.

Poor mangy Barr Wabbit didn't know what to do,
Trying to please the Golden Ferret put him into a real stew.*

---

*On May 2, 2019, Attorney General, William Barr, refused to testify before a
House Committee after being grilled by a Senate Committee the day before.

"Barr Wabbit Balances the Meuller Report"
by: Gnelia

SUBPOENA STEW

The large, long table was set for lunch,
The invited guests were sleepy and hunched.

Suddenly the alarm rang right on cue,
The host shouted, "it's time for some Subpoena Stew."

But what's this?
Who's refusing this simmering soupy bliss?

"Tis me, the White House Rabbit (Sarah Sanders)* that's who!"
"You'd be smart to take your lunch to Timbuktu."

"You'll not serve Subpoena Stew on these grounds,
As long as our Bloviator-in-Chief is still around."

"You see, he can't digest Subpoena Stew,
It makes him sick and have smelly Do Do."

"Well, if you continue to refuse,
You'll be in contempt if that is what you choose."

"Why don't you sit down and join our affair,
You'll enjoy the company of (John Bolton) the March Hare."

"The Door Mouse (Wilbur Ross)* is here half awake
He will only awaken for double Chocolate Cake."

Also, you will enjoy the floating (Steve Mnuchin)* Cheshire Cat,
With his sparkling teeth and a half moon smile under his MAGA
hat.

As for me, your wonderful host,
"I will chat with you and make a toast."

Clang, clang, my tick tock clock says time to stir my stew,
Smell the aroma of my chunky brew.

White House Rabbit what did you throw in my pot?
Looks like fake news investigative rot.

Are you trying to prevent me from serving my stew,
By making it a distasteful lumpy ragu?

You question the authenticity of my recipe,
Using unfounded allegations of impropriety?

It is a familiar ploy,
Used by dolts like you, so don't act coy.

I will not be thrown off course,
I shall ride honesty's white horse.

If the Bloviator-in-Chief chokes and spits out my stew from his
lippy mouth,
It will still have served its purpose to flush the truth out.

---

*Sarah Sanders was Trump's press front person known for her unrelenting support of Trump and his policies

*Wilbur Ross is Trump's Secretary of Commerce. When appointed he was 81 years old and has a sleepy appearance.

*Steve Mnuchin is Trump's Treasury Secretary who has an obvious devious grin.

TRUMP'S LOVEFEST WITH HIS SWEETIE
KIM JONG-UN

Ain't he sweet,
Just walking down the street.

My love for him has increased,
As we exchange fetching tweets.

Don't you like our slick hairdos,
Lots of grease rubbed with sinful glue.

We like to rub bellies,
And slap each other where we shake like jelly.

Yes, that's my man Kim,
I have professed love tor him.

It is hard to hear his reply,
Because he snorts like a pig when I look him in the eye.

But that 's OK because I'm fond of all dictators,
We all belong to an exclusive group of world HATERS.

TRUMP'S MAKE A DEAL STRATEGY

Whaddaya mean they won't sell!
I'll put maximum pressure on them or they can go to hell!

That's also my take on international diplomacy,
Just like my real estate experience until my numerous
bankruptcies.

Iran will cave if they know what's good for them,
I want their real estate in my Trump corporate pen.

Ah shucks, they shot down our drone!
But that doesn't matter, soon Iran will be my new foreign home.

For I will squeeze their Supreme Leader's purse,
Then he will kneel before me until his knees hurt.

Using the nuclear issue as an excuse,
I will get my way with this clever ruse.

Obama's deal was a real flop,
I will fix Iran's nuclear ambitions using my rhetorical mop.

Swish, swish here and a bucket of praise there,
I will cajole those Iranians to believing I really care.

Then, after I made my great deal they will suddenly realize,
Against me, they can't roll better than "snake eyes".

RAWHIDE

Rawhide, round'em up, slap slap, yipppeee,
Deport those miserable immigrants quickly.

As for those four female congresswomen of color,
Send them back to their shit-hole lands where life is crueler.

We don't need slacker immigrants,
And uppity congressional discontents.

The idea that members of congress would question me
is absurd.
Only I can run the country, not those lady nerds.

After rounding up the illegals, I will build a big running wheel
cage,
Then put them all in it on a large stage.

Where my followers can yell scorn,
While the illegals run for their lives until morn.

Only then would I consider amnesty for the survivors,
Because they would be prime candidates for labor camp driver

Trump announced that there would be a "mass raid" to round up illegal immigrants on
July 14, 2019.

OLD McCONNELL HAD A FARM

Old McConnell had a farm,
E-I-ee-I-o.

And on that farm he had a Pompeo pig,
E-i-ee-i-o.

With a snort, snort here,
And a snort, snort there.

Here a snort,
There a snort,

Everywhere a snort, snort,
Old McConnell had a farm.

And on that farm he had a tweeting Jackass,
E-i-ee-i-o.

With a tweet, tweet here,
And a tweet, tweet there,

Everywhere a tweet, tweet,
Old McConnell had farm.

On on that farm he had a Graham duck,
E-i-ee-i-o.

With a quack, quack here,
And a quack, quack there.

Everywhere a quack, quack,
Old McConnell had a farm.

And on that farm he had a Conway Chicken,
E-i-ee-i-o.

With a cluck cluck here,
And a cluck cluck there.

Everywhere a cluck, cluck,
Old McConnell had a farm.

And on that farm he had a Ross Opossum,
E-i-ee-i-o.

With a ZZZZ here,
And a ZZZZ there.
Everywhere a ZZZZZZZZ,
Old McConnell had a farm.

And on that farm he had a Mnuchin Snake,
E-i-ee-i-o.

With a hiss, hiss here,
And a hiss, hiss there.

Everywhere a hiss, hiss,
Old McConnell had a farm.

And on that farm he had a Pence Poodle,
E-i-ee-i-o.

With a pee, pee here,
And a pee, pee there.

Everywhere a pee, pee,
Old McConnell had a farm.

And on that farm he had a Hannity Horse,
E-i-ee-i-o.

With neigh, neigh here,
And a neigh, neigh there.

Everywhere a neigh, neigh,
Old McConnell had a farm.

And on that farm he had a Putin Porcupine,
E-i-ee-i-o.

With a prick, prick here,
And a prick, prick there.

Everywhere a prick, prick,
Old McConnell had a farm.

And on that farm he had a Barr Rat,
E-i-ee-i-o.

With a sniff, sniff here,
And a sniff, sniff there.

Everywhere a sniff, sniff,
Old McConnell had a farm.

And on that farm he had a Kavanaugh Kangaroo,
E-i-ee-i-o.

With hops (beer), hops here
And hops, hops there.

Everywhere hops, hops,
Old McConnell had a farm.

GREENLAND

"Buy Greenland!" bellows our fuzz-topped orange President,
We need a new immigrant pen for alien residents.

An iceberg wall,
Will surround them all,

Their children can pull sleds,
Like dogs before they go to bed.

We won't lose track of asylum seekers,
They will stay inside to warm their sneakers.

No swimming of rivers to worry about,
The invasive hordes will even have to crack ice for trout.

ANTI-TRUMP CHANT

(Modeled after his disgusting "lock her up" chant against Hillary Clinton)

Trump's juices flow with racist hate,
The crowd yells, MOP HIM UP, MOP HIM UP!

Each of his sentences stink of lies,
MOP HIM UP, MOP HIM UP!

All he cares about is being cute and demeaning,
MOP HIM UP, MOP HIM UP!

When your bucket is full of Trump Boastful Bigotry goop,
Throw it in the bin of horse shit poop.
MOP HIM UP, MOP HIM UP!

Then, again grab your mop for the next lie to drop,
Repeating, MOP HIM UP, MOP HIM UP!

SECRET AFGHANISTAN PEACE TALKS CANCELLED

Afghanistan President Ashraf Ghani, Taliban leaders, and me,
Were going to have such a lovely party for everyone to see,

Sunning ourselves amongst Camp David's old trees,
We would have sipped on bongs filled with tea.

The Taliban would have stayed at Mar A Lago on the ninth hole,
Afghan President Ghani would have bunked by the old flagpole.

I would have flown them to the US on our military jets,
Fueling on the way near my resorts at my request.

But darn, the old Taliban had to spoil it all,
By killing another US soldier this fall.

Our meeting had one detractor,
John Bolton was against it for many factors.

Secretary Mike Pompous Peo liked the idea,
Encouraging my suggestion with gushing verbal diarrhea.

Too bad I had to cancel our soiree,
Melania was going to be elegant for all eyes to see.

We would have chummed it up and shined our putters,
Never know what can happen when guys get together and share
talk from the gutter.

Oh well, start the killing again because I will blame Obama,
I've washed my hands of his incompetent drama.

On September 7, 2019, Trump announced he had cancelled secret peace talks between himself, the Taliban, and Afghan President Ashraf Ghani. The talks were to have occurred at Camp David. A loud out cry of disapproval erupted as it would have been close to the anniversary of 911 and leaders of the Taliban, our enemies, would have been on US soil.

CAMP TRUMP

Hello campers, hope you have a fine day,
Camp Trump offers many activities for your wonderful stay.

Today, we will have crafts in Melania's Village,
A prize given for the best Trump "chosen one" image.

Later canoe races at the DC swamp,
So grab your Pelosi Paddles to give her a whomp!

Tomorrow archery is our quest,
Sharpen your fiery barbed tweet arrows to meet the test.

Later we will have a tug of war,
Between our magnificent haters and our beloved NRA Corps.

Remember, the campfire will be followed by bedtime treats,
Yummy s'mores, distraction marshmallows, and chocolate
deceit.

On the last day we will have the first game of "Fake News",
So everyone bring their loud voices to express their anti-media
views.

Sadly, we soon will say goodbye to our emboldened trainees,
Having taught them to bring "reasoned" opinion to its knees.

LUNACY

On June 27, 2019, Trump told reporters "it's none of your business what he talks to Putin about."

On June 28, 2019, with Putin at his side, Trump casually joked to Putin, "Don't meddle in our election, please."

On June 28, 2019, Trump asked Putin if he had "Fake News" in his country. To which Putin said, "We also have."

On June 30, 2019, Trump stepped over the North/South Korean border at the DMZ to greet Kim Jong-un. In attendance was Moon Jae-in, President of South Korea. Trump jumped over the Moon?

On June 30, 2019, Trump claimed Obama was begging for a meeting with Kim Jong-un but was rebuffed by Kim. "That is a lie", according to two top Obama aides. "It was the other way around as Obama and other past presidents wouldn't meet with Kim as long as he was pursuing nuclear weapons."

In July 2019, England's US Ambassador described Trump as "inept" and "incompetent" in cables he sent to his superiors in England.

TEETER TOTTER

Up and down we go,
Rising up and down, to and fro.

Holding that scene in your mind,
Think of politicians doing their daily grind.

Teeter tottering on the board of truth,
Going up and down, tearing it from its roots.

Pushing their opponent down while they go up,
In retaliation, their opponent does the same accusing him of
being corrupt.

The truth beam never stays even,
Wildly pushing each other up and down, what are we to believe
in?

Then all of a sudden the truth beam cracks,
Giving Truth a heart attack.

If it is broken,
Truth will never be spoken.

In the furious up and downs,
Both have lost their angelic crowns.

Even though one may be close to the truth,
He/she accuses the other of being a liar and uncouth.

So it begins all over again,
Up and down, over and over, making us go insane.

UKRANIAN WALTZ

Hello, Volodymyr Zelensky*, this is your favorite President,
You know the one holding back all your armaments.

Yes, it is time for your country to pay the piper,
For, without the US, your poor country still would be diapered.

So, before I give you more aid and war tools,
I need a "favor" about info on my political opponent fool.

Yes, it is as you think,
Joe Biden and his son Hunter, the Dink.

Seems as though Hunter was corrupt in your land,
And that "Sleepy Joe" gave him a hand.

Your courageous Prosecutor-General, Viktor Shokin, was bold,
He had Hunter Biden in his sights I am told.

But he was fired at "Sleepy's" request,
So I need to know more about this corrupt mess.

You will help me, won't you, "Volody", to root out the sleaze,
Just for me, old pal, pretty please.

Now, wait a minute, why are you hesitating at my request?
May I remind you of who is holding your war chest.

Because if you don't dig up this dirt,
I will see to if you don't get any aid, you "little squirt".

I am the one holding the cards,
Without me you will go back to comedy skits in backyards.

I am sending to Ukraine my Attorney, Rudy "the Striker",
To get the "Biden" dirt from your Prosecutor tiger.

Feel free to tell him everything nasty,
He used to be New York's Mayor, so he's no patsy.

---

*Volodymyr Zelensky was elected as President of the Ukraine in May 2019. He was a former actor and comedian. In a July 25, 2019, phone call Trump is reported to have asked Zelensky for a "favor". This request was for information on Joe Biden and his son Hunter. Pending at the time was a grant of aid to the Ukraine that was passed by the Senate and House but Trump had held up. This call led to the formal request for a formal impeachment inquiry to be conducted by the US House of Representatives.

COME OUT WHOEVER YOU ARE!

Like a deer in the headlights out of control,
Like a rabbit in a frenzy searching for its hole.

Trump is pulling nasty words for the whistleblower out of the sky,
Even going so far as suggesting he/she is a spy.*

He demands to meet the whistleblower face to face,
Such crazy talk usually is reserved for a wing nut case.

But there he goes in full view,
Never bashful about his sick spew.

The impeachment train is leaving the station,
Soon it will be gripping the nation.

Will Trump stop it on its tracks?
Or will he be run over in spite of his attacks?

Doubtful he will be able to live up to the task,
As he routinely drags his words out of his ass.

In September 2019, after the revelation of the whistleblower complaint, Trump
suggested the whistleblower was a spy.

WACK A DOODLES
(started in rhyme but overwhelmed by events)

Trump said he runs the country, *
Acting like this is elementary.

Trump tweeted he met with the Prince of "Whales",
Then tried to delete the incorrect spelling to no avail. *

Beginning June 24, 2019, Trump said, in a ghoulish rant,
ICE is going to round up millions of illegal immigrants.

Not knowing what he was talking about,
The Dept. of Homeland Security freaked out. *

On June 19, 2019, Iran shot down a US drone, *
"Wasn't intentional", Trump says with a groan.

But he says Iran made a "big mistake" by doing so,
And his response we would soon know.

Then he approved an Iran attack,
But when planes were warming up he called them back.

Then Trump cancelled the illegal immigrant "mass arrests",
Giving the Democrats two weeks to fix the asylum mess.

---

*On the Fourth of July 2019, in his speech from the Lincoln Memorial, Trump praised George Washington's Revolutionary Army for "taking over" the airports during America's Revolutionary War.

*On July 23, 2019, Donald Trump said that pursuant to Article 2 of the Constitution, he can do anything he wants as President.

*On July 27, 2019, Trump tweeted that Elijah Cumming's district in Maryland is "considered the Worst in the USA", a disgusting, rat infested mess," a very dangerous & filthy place." "No human being would want to live there."

*On July 30, 2019, Trump said, "The people in Baltimore are living in Hell."

*On August 15, 2019, Trump railed that because the economy is going so great, "you have no choice but to vote for me because your 401 K accounts would go down the tubes.

*On August 13, 2019, Trump told a rally at a Petro Chemical plant in Pennsylvania that if their Union leaders don't support him, vote them out of office.

*On August 18, 2019, Trump said his trade war with China is not affecting the US, only China. "We are doing tremendously well, our consumers are rich, I gave a tremendous tax cut, and they are loaded with money."

*On August 20, 2019, Trump said that Jews who vote Democratic are disloyal.

*On August 21, 2019, Trump said 1.) He is the "chosen one" to bring China to a trade agreement. 2.) He wants Russia to again join the G-7 even though they were kicked out for its invasion of the Crimea. 3.) He said Putin out smarted Obama on Crimea. 4.) He said that the Danish Prime Minister was «nasty» when she called Trump›s offer to buy Greenland as «absurd». 5) He re-tweeted a conspiracy theorist statement that Trump was the King of Israel and the "Second coming of God", thanking him for those compliments. 6.) He repeated his claim that votes for Democrats are disloyal to Israel and the Jewish people. 7.) That he may have to release thousands of ISIS fighters, currently being held by a US backed group in Syria, back to where they came from, France and Germany, unless those countries repatriate them.

*On August 23, 2019, Trump queried, "who is the bigger enemy, Jay Powell or Chairman Xi"? This came after China retaliated with tariffs and Trump retaliated back. With looming economic uncertainty, Trump is displeased that Fed. Chairman Powell hasn't lowered interest rates.

*On August 23, 2019, Trump ordered US Companies to find alternative countries with which to do business rather than China.

*In August 2019, when Hurricane Dorian was approaching Puerto Rico, Trump said, "Puerto Rico is one of the most corrupt places on earth". He also derided the mayor of the island's largest city, San Juan, as "incompetent"."

*In August 2019, Trump joked about trading Puerto Rico for Greenland.

*On September 4, 2019, in attempting to explain the possible path of Hurricane Dorian, Trump drew a semi-circle addition with a Sharpie on a NOAA map to include Alabama, where forecasters did not expect the hurricane to land. Confronted by this false projection, Trump claimed he didn›t know who did it but continued to argue Alabama was in Dorian›s path even though NOAA disputed this claim.

*In August 2019, Trump suggested dropping nuclear bombs on hurricanes to stop them from hitting the USA.

*On September 12, 2019, Trump said he would roll back regulations on power-saving light bulbs because they make him look orange. He prefers the old incandescent bulbs as they emit better light.

*On September 29, 2019, Trump tweeted that if he was impeached there would be a Civil War-like fracture that the country would not recover from.

FIDDLE DEE DEE

So take that Pelosi, you hag,
I'm not allowing my staff to talk to you, so pack your bag.

Your impeachment inquiry is a rotten hoax,
Can be seen through even by ordinary folks.

My shadow minions led by Jim, the "Jackel" Jordan,*
Will savage holes in your secrecy curtain.

* Jim Jordan is an Ohio Congressman who is a fervent Trump supporter.

TURKEY VS. KURDISTAN BOXING MATCH

In the right corner wearing the white flag trunks is Treasonous
Trump.
In the opposite corner not wearing any trunks is Pinky Putin
"Rump".

As they approach the center of the ring,
The Referee says US troops will score this thing.

Unfair cries Pinky "Rump",
"I agree", says Treasonous Trump.

"Whatever Pinky says is fine with me,
I command my troops to get out of here and flee."

"Pinky and I agree Turkey's Erdogan is a fine man,
He is strong and has a magnificent plan."

"His plan to clean out twenty miles of Kurds along the Turkey's
border,
Sounds reasonable to both of us to restore order."

"The Kurds are no angels after all,
So what if they have been killed in our ISIS brawl."

Ding, ding goes the ringside bell,
Both fighters hit their gloves and dance as if in a spell,

"All right you win Pinky, my bone spurs are acting up",
"Your troops can fill the void so drink from the winners cup."*

"Wait a minute", shouts the sparse crowd,
"The US is withdrawing hidden in a loser's shroud?"

"No, no", shouts Treasonous Trump "it is a great victory",
"No one could have done what I just did with my sly trickery."

"I am joining my retreating troops, leaving Pinky with his spoils,
Along with Turkish towels and bath oils".

"Who needs to be in the ring with Pinky,
He will take on the Turks and Kurds so we won't get stinky."

"As I promised in my campaign.
Our troops will come home and drink victory Champagne."

"Doesn't matter if our Kurd war pals get bloody,
"My way or the highway", is my mantra for my swamp buggy".

76

*On October 17, 2019, Trump announced a five-day ceasefire between Turkey and the Kurds. Turkey denied that it was a ceasefire but only a "pause". In the meantime the withdrawal of US troops continued as Trump announced on October 6, 2019. That left a Twenty Mile stretch of Kurdish territory in the hands of the Turks. Trump received worldwide condemnation along with criticism from many members of his own Republican party for his order to remove US troops from this area.

MULVANEY, THE HOOTING IMPEACHMENT OWL

There once was a man named Mulvaney,
Who spoke like an owl with no brainy.

He hooted the truth to reporters,*
But then he retracted his words with retorters.

Me oh my, what have I done in my hoots?
I've created scandal standing there in my boots.

I admitted an impeachable offense done by my boss,
What will he say? Will I get tossed?

All I said was already known, done time and time again,
Get over it, done all the time, hold back aid for political gain.

Yes sir, I spoke forthrightly, you know,
No aid for Ukraine unless they give 2016 US election info.

Now I realize Trump got upset,
So I went back to my nest.

I reversed my earlier hoots with more flavorful herbs,
And denying my beak spoke those words.

But alas, my hoots may add to Trump's impeachment inquiry,
Just like my fellow bureaucratic owls' words in their diaries.

---

*On October 17, 2019, Mr. Mulvaney, White House Chief of Staff, admitted in a press
conference that one of the conditions of Ukraine receiving US military aid was that
Ukraine had to help the US investigate corruption related to the 2016 US election. He
remarked that this type of political request is done all the time and for us to get over it.

PRESIDENT GUESS WHO?

Once upon a time there was a President
Who lived in a Poison Oak tree.

His poison leaked and leaked,
As far as anyone could see,

Then one day he started itching from inside out,
Making no sense in words from his mouth.

Alarmed, he put his hands down his large snout,
Then crammed in his feet and wiggled them all about.

To his fright he couldn't pull them back,
Making it easy for his enemies to attack.

He tried to speak coherently but to no avail,
It was then he realized he had become a human snail.

With his hunched back in the air,
And having no arms or legs he created quite a stare.

He could only move slowly by sliding on his slimy spit,
Not like he used to go, lickety-split.

To persuade his followers to keep the faith,
He perfumed his frothy slime to disguise its vicious taste.

So he now slithers from town to town,
Spreading his vitriolic secretions all around.

SONG FROM AMERICA'S MOUTH

Zip-a-dee-doo-dah, Zip-a-dee-ay,
The Impeachment Inquiry is finally underway.

Uga Chaka, Uga Chaka

Yeah, Yeah, Yeah,
My o my what a wonderful Day!

Uga Chaka, Uga Chaka Yippee Di Ay

BULLSHIT

Today, 10-2-19, I announced the Democrats are throwing
Bullshit* at me,
You may think my words are un-presidential but that is up to me.

I am the decider and emperor all rolled into one,
So, stand aside while this so-called impeachment becomes fun.

The Democrats are led by, "Shifty Schiff",
Who couldn't carry Pompeo's Jockstrap* even with an easy lift.

Then there are the Bidens, "STONE COLD CROOKED",
So rotten, they won't even stay on fishing hooks.

You know, I just don't need the Ukraine,
To bring Hunter and "Sleepy" Joe Biden pain.

I told China to bring me their heads,*
They will bring me corrupt information the Bidens will dread.

It may be unlawful for me to ask foreigners to dig up dirt,
But I don't care, even if the "dirt" is fake, just so it hurts.

---

*On October 2, 2019, Trump accused the Democrats of pursuing "BULLSHIT" against
him for impeachment. He also made the "jockstrap" comment on this same day
concerning Representative Adam Schiff who is the head of the House Intelligence
Committee. On the same day Trump called Joe and Hunter Biden "Stone Cold Crooked"

*On October 3, 2019, Trump publicly asked China to help investigate Joe and Hunter
Biden.

NOW FOR THE REST OF THE STORY

The cast: Donald J. Trump, AKA "Big Fingers Don" or "BFD" for short: Rudy Giuliani, AKA "Big Giulie" or "BG" for short.

The scene: The return of BG from the Ukraine after his further hunt for "dirt" on the Bidens. This occurred just as the House was finalizing its articles of impeachment against President Trump.

BFD: Whaddya got for me, "Big Giulie"?
BG: Big Fingers Don, you won't believe it, I found a Ukrainian stoolie.

BFD: I hope he/she has juicy dirt on Joe Biden as my ass is in distress,
BG: Don't worry I will get you out of your impeachment mess.

BFD: I hope so. I don't want Moscow Mitch to send me down that road.
BG: Relax, Big Fingers Don, my Slavic blonde bombshell will deliver the payload.

BFD: Oh no! Not another Stormy!
BG: No, No. This one has the goods, real gory.

BFD: I can hardly wait to hear,
BG: What I've got will clean out your ear.

BG: Here goes! Willy Wonka is at the center of this scheme.
BFD: Are you nuts? What does that mean?

BG: Well, it is scandalous. He conspired with Ukraine President Zelensky to control the Borscht soup market.
BFD: What? Shut up!

BG: Yes, to create a Chocolate/Borscht combination to win the Borscht world soup competition.
BFD: How does that help me bring down Biden into submission?

BG: Glad you asked. Hunter Biden sits on Wonka's factory
Board.
BFD: You mean the famous Chocolate Factory is involved in
something untoward?

BG: Right! And therefore Joe must also be involved in this
conspiracy.
BFD: Finally, I got Joe in the soup of misery.

BG: You just tell Zelensky no cabbage unless he investigates the
Bidens,
BFD: Great idea BG! He will bow before me frightened.

BFD: I will be famous for exposing the Soup conspiracy plot,
        That will send my 2020 opponent to rot.

"Big Giulie"
by: Luke

HALL OF SHAME

The Senate, once a revered body,
Has suddenly in the Trump impeachment become an oddity.

OK to resist subpoenas to testify,
Just give the finger to the House and say, "bye bye".

Images of Senators sleeping at the impeachment trial,
Went viral.

Senators don't care about the facts,
They just want a quick vote and to cover their tracks.

"We don't need witness testimony", they cry,
Our Roman Candle President wouldn't lie?

No matter if he was going after the Bidens,
"Not impeachable conduct, no reason to be frightened".

"No crime, no foul",
The GOP Senators howl.

Such epithets are not only untrue but hard to swallow,
What if Trump pardoned all murderers on death row?

Would this be an abuse of power? The GOP says, doesn't matter,
Just let him do it and watch those murderers scatter.

"No crime, no foul" is like a bad case of jock itch,
Its idiocy is as blatant as a shoe salesman's pitch.*

---

* During Trump's impeachment trial in the Senate some members were caught dozing off.   The Republicans argued that "Abuse of Power", as stated in the first Article of impeachment, cannot be a basis of impeachment. That impeachment can only be based on committing a crime. Also they argued that not obeying witness subpoenas was the right thing to do on the basis of claimed "executive privilege".

BEE IN TRUMP'S BONNET

Like a bee in my bonnet,
Conspiracy theories buzz in me like a beautiful sonnet.

I can't get them out of my mind,
I must find out if they are true and not designed.

Giuliani, my trusted servant, knows about corruption,
He keeps stirring it up without interruption.

I am in a frenzy and out of control,
Everything appears to be in a conspiracy sinkhole.

The press is corrupt and sells fake news,
All its reporters, except Fox, don't share my conspiracy views.

I must tap out my feelings on my twitter machine,
My thumbs fly, already knowing my words from the latrine.

I can't help myself, please someone intervene,
My hair is falling out and face losing its sheen.

Oh no, the curtain is opening and I must rally my crowd,
Please impeach me, save me from the lunacy shroud.

THE END OF IMPEACHMENT

Shut it down, Shut it down,
We don't need no stinking witnesses, they are just clowns.

We Imperial Senators can decide what's true,
We'll rub our crystal balls until they show our point of view.

Can't be an impeachment unless we say so,
Won't happen under our watch as Trump has us in tow.

We march to his commands, laughing at his jokes,
All the while pulling his chariot of corruption chained to our yokes.

His twitter machine "likes" feed us every day,
With idolizing fans behaving like jackasses braying for hay.

While these crazed voters recycle his vicious cud,
We continue to pull his chariot through the impeachment mud.

As we do so, those foolish voters put flowers in our hair,
Celebrating their "Savior" Trump with adoration flare.

Our effort becomes easier with every advance,
With all of us GOP Senators marching in a Nazi-like dance.

Nothing will stop us after winning this impeachment hoax,
Our gilded corruption chariot will roll over disbelieving folks.

So get out of the way and kneel to our golden leader,
Nothing can be done to our famous tweeter.

TRUMP SHOUTS "FREE AT LAST"

Free at last, free at last,
Thank God I am free at last,

I don't care about being impeached by the House,
I will spin my acquittal proclaiming I am as innocent as a church
mouse.

At my State of the Union Address my GOP comrades cheered,
Shouting my blessing by chanting "four more years".

Then, while still in a celebratory mood and sparing no spittle,
I let the Democrats have it the day after my acquittal.

I used my favorite word to describe the Democrats' crusade,
"BULLSHIT", I shouted to my adoring staff that I have already
swayed.

There is spring in my step as I address,
The annoying witch hunt fake news press.

As for Pelosi who tore up my "Gettysburg" like address,
She is a horrible person who should be treated like an invasive
pest.

My State of the Union address was truly a thing of beauty
In spite of SPEAKER Pelosi's act of unconscionable cruelty.*

On the day after my acquittal I thanked my adoring staff,
For their loyalty and acceptance of my propensity for graft.

At the end his speech Speaker Pelosi tore it up.

McCONNELL ON THE PROWL

Nit wit Mitch,
Moscow Mitch.

No matter what you call him,
He is a small hat without a brim.

With alley cat-like eyes,
He eats his prey no matter what its size.

One wonders what his diet will cause,
Will he shrivel up and blow away to our applause?

Or, will he continue to obstruct and tell lies,
Refueling from the political cadavers he ate before our eyes.

Why can we say he eats his opponents?
Just look at how he treats his fellow senators as rodents.

When he twitches his cat-like whiskers,
His eyes bug out with joy in his knickers.

He pounces and starts pulling his prey to his point of view,
Threatening to expose them using his rhetorical screws.

Once overcome and subdued,
His prey becomes his servant doing his bidding without a clue.

LEARNED HIS LESSON?

GOP Senators liked his repentant smile,
Thought he had learned his lesson from his impeachment trial.

But, lo and behold, his camouflaged hateful gut,
Emerged again after he was pardoned by the GOP Senate gang
of mutts.

Shouting to the Vindman twins «you are fired and don›t look
back»,*
Trump brought revenge, calling them political hacks.

He dismissed Gordon Sondland in a similar way,
Berating him, claiming he stood in his way.

In the wake of being impeached,
Trump is extending his powers beyond our reach.

Now with no sense of remorse,
Trump claims he can intervene in DOJ criminal cases and mount
the defendant's horse. *

Such unbridled abuse of power has never been seen,
Kicking dirt in our faces in tweets from his hate latrine.

---

*Immediately following his impeachment acquittal in the Senate Trump fired
Colonel Vindman and Gordon Sondland. Both had given damaging testimony against
Trump. He even fired the Colonel's brother who was not a participant in the trial.

Trump claimed the right to intervene in any DOJ criminal case after voicing his
displeasure with the DOJ sentencing recommendation in the Roger Stone case. Stone
is a longtime supporter of Trump.

PROTECT YOURSELF FROM THE TRUMP CON-VIRUS

Holy smokes!
Trump Con-virus* is spreading amongst ordinary folks.

People are warned to wear masks,
Making sure they have filters up to the task.

Flights to and from Mar-A-Lago are on a freeze,
Preventing the spread of this deadly disease.

Symptoms include loss of reason and common sense views,
Coupled with a fever and insatiable frenzy to watch Fox news.

Loss of friendships commonly occurs late,
Leaving their victims isolated, filled with hate.

Seeking a cure for their personal death valley,
They religiously attend raucous Trump rallies.

There, they are like the walking dead,
Mindlessly repeating whatever their Fuhrer has said.

In early 2020, a deadly virus originated in China and threatened to spread worldwide. It was named Corona Viral Disease (COVID) 19

CORONAVIRUS SONG

TO BE SUNG, HUMMED OR EVEN MUMBLED TO THE TUNE "CAMPTOWN RACES" BY STEPHEN FOSTER.

The novel Coronavirus is coming to town*,
Doo-da, doo-da,
Oh, de doo-da day.

Gonna infect us all night, gonna infect us all day,
Doo-da, doo-da,
Don't bet any money on a Trump cure, he didn't give Doctors any hay.*
Oh, de doo-da day

Says he is gonna give us all masks,
Doo-da, doo-da,
So we can continue our daily tasks,
Oh, de doo-da day

Out of the blue he appointed Sir Pence a Lot,
Doo-da, doo-da,
To lead the charge to kill the virus rot.
Oh, de doo-da day.

With a tsk tsk here and a tsk tsk there,
Doo-da, doo-da,
Everywhere a tsk tsk, Pence will lead us from his easy chair.
Oh, de doo-da day.

Meanwhile, at 4:00 AM Trump sits at his dining table,
Doo-da, doo-da,
Composing on twitter his Coronavirus fable.
Oh, de doo-da day.

With thousands of Americans quivering in fear,
Doo-da, doo-da,
He fondly polishes and strokes his golfing gear.
Oh, de doo-da day.

Trump irrationally proclaimed to all his folks,
Doo-da, doo-da,

"

This whole Coronavirus thing is just a Democrat hoax,
Oh, de doo-da day.

In typical Trump fashion he spins this virus saga,
Doo-da, doo-da,
He may even claim Obama created it to hurt him with the help of
Lady Gaga.
Oh, de doo-da day.

92

---

*In 2020, the Coronavirus spread from China and threatened people and economies around the world.

*In 2018, the CDC had to cut 80% of its efforts to prevent global disease outbreaks because it was running out of money. It went from working in 49 countries to just 10. Trump administration shut down the entire global health-security unit of the National Security Council. It reduced national health spending by $15 billion. It eliminated the United States $30 million Complex Crises Fund. (Business Insider 2-25-20)

NEW SHERIFF IN TOWN

Once upon a time a big, bad, mean virus came to town,
Townsfolk prepared to meet this threat and not back down.

But one of the elders made the case,
To see the new Sheriff, just in case.

So off they went to the Sheriff's Mar A Lago retreat,
To see if he would get the big, bad, mean Virus off the street.

The new Sheriff had just replaced the popular two-term one,
Now is the time for him to rise to the occasion to be the favorite son.

"Sheriff we need your help", pleaded the Mayor of the town,
There is a big, bad, mean virus about to mow us down."

"Don't worry little ones", the Sheriff proclaimed,
That old virus will be in my aim."

"Now go away, I need to make my tee time at the first hole,
I'll figure out something that will be big and bold".

"Relax as you go back to town,
That big, bad, mean virus will be gone by sundown."

"I know a lot about diseases, I am the smartest guy in the room,
I am gifted to know what to do in these times of gloom."

"I know from my vast experience it will go away like a miracle,
It will go away when warm weather comes, so don't get hysterical."

"I just found out that there is a posse of leeches headed our way,
Word is that they can kill viruses in less than a day."

"This could be a 'game changer' for the future of the world,*
If it does, I will stand tall with my victorious Trump cape unfurled."

During the Coronavirus pandemic Trump persistently expressed hope that certain older Malaria drugs could be a "game changer" in fighting the Coronavirus.

ECONOMY NEEDS SACRIFICAL LIVES

Remember the virgins sacrificed to King Kong,
Now Trump wants to sacrifice senior citizens to the virus that's
become so strong.*

Trump wants the economy to burst ahead,
He says it can't do that if it remains in a shed.

He contends the young are likely to survive this disease,
So feed the seniors to the virus to give the rest of us a reprieve.

As the seniors' ashes simmer,
Let the economic gods through the gates for a steak dinner.

Sure, the rich, like him, may get richer,
What does he care if workers get sicker.

Trump claims we are ahead of the grim reaper,
Just in time for a celebration at Easter.

Christ's resurrection may be the reason for the day,
But the economy will give Trump the reason to make political
hay.

Even though the virus continues to rage across the land,
Trump wants the US economic engine to resume with all hands.

Saying the US economy wasn't created to be shutdown,
He thinks, against medical evidence that the virus war has been
won.

In a macabre statement he forecast many suicides from
depression,
If the nation doesn't avoid a financial virus-caused recession.

So die at work from the virus on behalf of the nation,
Or die of suicide at home from virus isolation.

Along with the massive aid to be given to companies,
Shoving us back to work will help feed their corporate gluttony.

Trump's corporate buddies will reap millions from his aid,
As we Americans suffer, he drinks Coca Cola in the Florida
shade.

* On March 24, 2020, as the curve of infections from the Coronavirus trended upward, Trump declared he wanted restrictions on group gatherings and employment due to the virus lifted by April 12, 2020, Easter Sunday.

The Republican Lt. Governor of Texas said as a senior citizen he would trade his vulnerability to the virus for the younger generation to economically succeed and therefore return to work in spite of social distancing to prevent the spread of the virus.

On March 24, 2020, Trump predicted mass suicides from depression as a result of financial difficulties caused by economic stresses from the virus.

NONESSENTIAL* RAG

All right. Dancers gather round,
Time to do the "nonessential rag" that's sweeping the town.

Now all those essential guys and gals have a chair,
It's time for us nonessentials to have some flair.

Hold your partner tight and swing to the left,
Do the same to the right billowing your lady's dress.

Tap your feet, jump up and down,
Snap your face mask, spin your partner round.

Sneeze your spittle away from the circle,
Do-si-do then Mud Turtle.

Stay six feet apart, the social distance measure,
Lifting your arms while swaying with rhythmic gesture.

Now with intensity and ferocity,
Sharpen your curve with upward velocity.

Exhausted at your apex you will be want to retire,
But slide down the other side as you perspire.

Easy now, slow down your pace,
Nonessentials, saunter back home, you know your place.

---

*During the Coronavirus Pandemic it was directed by most State governments that all nonessential workers stay home.

TRUMP, THE NOT SO FUNNY CLOWN

Clarabell the Clown would never use a stinger,
But that is what Clown Trump uses as he tosses his zingers.

Just as the Coronavirus spreads across the land,
He continues to castigate anyone speaking ill of his stands.

Especially directed at the news media expressing concerns,
About his initial weak virus response, rebutting in
vigorous terms.*

With his jaw jutting forward and red/orange complexion ablaze,
He lashes at the press in a blustery haze.

Standing like a school boy having received a tongue lashing,
He responds with a volcanic verbal gnashing.

In his mind he must get the better of any critique,
Doing otherwise, his Daddy would have considered him very
weak.

Portraying himself as the "best" at any endeavor,
He deflects and parries by attempting to be clever.

It is sadly becoming a regular show,
Routinely giving the press a "blow".

Unlike Clarabell the Clown laughingly honking at Howdy Doody,*
Clown Trump maliciously honks his tweeter rudely.

Looking deep inside his clown suit,
There is no joy, just poisonous fruit.

---

*On March 19 and 20, 2020, in the midst of a press conferences about
the Coronavirus, Mr. Trump went on a tirade against the press for their coverage of his
response to the Coronavirus Pandemic. He called NBC reporter Peter Alexander a
terrible reporter for a mundane question asking him to respond to Americans scared by
the pandemic.

*For those unfamiliar with "Howdy Doody" and his partner "Clarabell the Clown", the
latter was a mute who communicated by honking his horn and occasionally spraying
seltzer.

"Blaster of Tweets"
by: Sol

SPACE FORCE TALK

Dialogue between Captain Hot Jock (Trump) and Co-Pilot
Snowball (Pence) after the 2016 Presidential Election nearing the
2020 election:

"Not much doing out here today, Captain, quite a snoozer.
Do you think by nightfall we will make the planet 'Hillary',
AKA 'the loser'."

"Sure we will, nothing can stop our new space force, *
Remember, Snowball, just like golf, drive our balls straight down
the course."

"So, correctly set our route at warp speed,
Watching out for anything in our path that will impede."

"Pardon me Captain, where did you get the name, 'Hot Jock'?"
Well, remember Old Buck Jeffery Epstein* with his wavy locks?"

"Buck and I did the town up brown one night and day,
Of course, I outlasted him in our pleasure play."

"I am the favorite, you know, with the barroom crowds,
 Maidens that surround me would make you proud."

"How did you get to be a Space Captain?
You must have had a resume polished like satin."

"I proved myself as a leader by conviction,
Making money in real estate, tossing out tenants in mass
evictions."

"No matter how they screamed and had rags on their feet,
I threw them out along with their shabby belongings into the
street."

"My stone-faced approach caught the Republicans' eye,
They said, 'we can work with this guy'."

"Then came the election, you as the Christian angel and me,
being crude,

We fooled the entire nation into believing the crap that we spewed."

"Anyway, I digress. Snowball what is our status?"
Mine is fine but you have (pee-yew) flatus."

"Oh no, Coronavirus-19 is still heading our way,
This is going to throw off our plans for a victory election day."

"Quick, set us at operation warp speed, *
Initially, I pooh-poohed it, now they will say I tried to mislead."

"We are just going to take the hit and wish the effects away,
Just like we made up stuff before, we'll do it again my way."

"But Captain Hot Jock, do you think we can do it again?"
"Sure, Snowball, it's easy, just lie and make up a cure regimen.

"Don't believe science, as it's beyond our fans intellectual reach,
Just say, 'the virus can be cured by drinking bleach'."

"The problem, Snowball, is that your hair will turn yellow,
And together we will look like an Orange with Lemon Jello."

---

* Jeffery Epstein was a convicted sex offender who hung out frequently with Trump. He committed suicide while awaiting trial on sex charges.

* After finally recognizing the severity of the Coronavirus epidemic, Trump announced that he was creating operation Warp Speed to create a vaccine.

* Trump created a separate military agency called the "Space Force".

"No News Like Bad News"
by: Carson and Leela-Jean

DR. WHO

No more assistance for the World Health Organization,
I will eliminate WHO with financial castration.*

It failed even after getting all our dough,
My fabulous brain knows more than it will ever know.

I, Trump, am the Doctor of the World that's for sure,
Only I know the prescription for a Coronavirus cure.

Bleach combined with UV rays is my remedy,*
To kill the Coronavirus malady.

Just take your daily dose of bleach,
Fill a thermos and take it at the beach.

My potion will flush your Coronavirus away,
Down through your intestines and out your rear doorway.

So drink bleach and tan to your heart's content,
What have you got to lose in this perilous moment.*

Because it also functions as a bowel cleanse,
My new hat slogan will be "Make America Shit Again.

---

*On April 14, 2020, Trump announced he is suspending the US funding for WHO.

* On April 23, 2020, Trump suggested studying the idea of ingesting and/or injecting disinfectants into the body as a cure for the Coronavirus. He also suggested UV waves from sunlight as a possible cure.

* While continuing to recommend alternative unproven remedies for the Coronavirus, Trump repeatedly stated, "what have you got to lose".

DEATH VALLEY DAYS

Remember the Death Valley Days show,
Featuring the "Old Ranger" sponsored by Boraxo?

Some of you young 'uns might not.
But us oldsters, we watched it a lot.

The Boraxo 20 mule team would plod across open space,
Then the "Old Ranger" would show his gnarled face.

The show would begin in our TV machine,
With a new adventure that glued our eyes to the shimmering
screen.

Somehow, this show comes to mind,
As President Trump gives his advice, leaving science behind.

The title of the show is befitting of the Coronavirus scourge,
Trump is presiding over our "Death Valley" purge.

Maybe it is the Boraxo cleanser that makes me think,
When Trump says drink disinfectant from under our sinks.

The "Old Ranger" is a good name for Trump,
But the real one was pleasant, not dumb as a stump.

Trump has a mule team-like cabinet of fools,
That eats from his verbal feedbag and wipes his drools

Behind the scene, his jackass team's whip is snapping,
Trying to control Trump's wagon tongue from insanely flapping.

CALMING BALM

In crisis, President Franklin Roosevelt calmed the nation with Fireside Chats,
In contrast, Donald Trump had daily briefings with fiery press spats.

Sinking to even a new low, Trump digressed,
"Sue the ass off" the informant who led to his impeachment mess. *

These types of sudden breaks in his thinking,
Show the process of mental thinning.

While repeatedly calling the news media "fake",
He tried to cheerlead the country from the Coronavirus snake.

Claiming ultimate authority over the States,
He said he is the only person who can open the economic gates.

"I am the President, no one can do it other than me, *
I will stop the "stay at home" orders in spite of any Governor's decree".

"After all, in my wisdom, I knew the pandemic was coming,
Only I know when again our businesses will start humming".

"My cheerleading is endearing to the masses,
My hotels need virus-ridden workers to get off their asses".

"Just like Moses made the Red Sea part,
I will turn this Chinese Virus into a fragrant fart."

---

*On April 4, 2020, Trump said someone should sue the ass off the informant who led to his impeachment trial.

On April 13, 2020, Trump claimed to have the ultimate authority to decide when the US economy could be reopened and social restrictions lifted after the Coronavirus subsides.

WHAT THE HELL!

June 1, 2020, was an interesting day, for out of his hole,
President Trump went for a stroll.

Along with his entourage of cabinet clones,
Who marched like robots following instructions on their
headphones.

This robotic walk was made during police brutality protests,
About the killing of George Floyd that sparked civil unrest.*

While peaceful protests were going on he chose to go,
Just down the street from his White House bungalow.

To historic St. John's Episcopal Church,
For a photo-op displaying a Bible in front of his girth.

There he stood silently with the Bible upside down,
Stone-faced, with his trademark scowl that resembles a frown.

Turning and pivoting with the Bible in hand,
He attempted to appeal to the religious right across the land.

Was his statuesque Bible pose to make protesters kneel without
a sermon?
By pretending to be a Christ-like healer of all men?

Can't imagine Jesus on the Mount with followers at his feet,
Just holding scriptures and staring, with no words to speak.

Just what religious message was he trying to convey,
Using the Bible with nothing meaningful to say?

His silence was deafening to the event at hand,
While civil unrest was sweeping the land.

To even get to the Church for use as his podium,
Protesters were gassed and shoved causing pandemonium.

Scoundrel Trump's Bible-holding image scorched our land,
It is a wonder that the Bible didn't burn a hole in his hand.

---

* On May 25, 2020, George Floyd, a Black man, was killed by a Minneapolis Police
Officer who had placed his knee on Floyd's neck as he lay on the ground.

TRUMP'S GARDEN OF HEROES

A botanical setting full of skunkweeds,
Reflecting not history but Trump's psychological needs.

Sean Hannity›s face is on the opening gate,
With Laura Ingraham's bust looming above a man-made lake.

Commentators from Fox News,
Are depicted everywhere in visitors' views.

A Rupert Murdoch fountain statue,
Squirts a stream of yellow journalism pew.

A shaded lane leads to a giant throne,
On which sits Trump's pal, Roger Stone.

Gardeners, painstakingly carved an image,
Of his father, Fred Trump, looking smug and privileged.

Rush Limbaugh's profile is etched on the men's bathroom walls,
Above the urinals and commode stalls.

Sanitary wipe dispensers throughout the park,
Have Moscow Mitch's eyes that glow in the dark.

Amongst the various souvenir nick nacks,
Ivanka's silhouette appears on pairs of mud flaps.

A Trump tower rises in the center of this disgusting place,
Capped by a giant revolving red MAGA hat with Trump's face.

Only fast food is served in this crazy like zoo,
Drink containers in small print show Melania's "BE BEST" views.

Lastly, there is a petting corral at the exit stop.
Where Supreme Court nominees are fed right wing slop.

---

*On July 3, 2020, in the shadow of Mount Rushmore Trump proposed building a
National Garden of Heroes.

FOUR AM PILLOW TALK

"Wake up Melania, get comfortable, take a pee,
The fourth rerun of my Coronavirus press conference is on TV."

"I am so smooth before the cameras,
Notice my sarcastic tone and glowing orange stamina."

Clenching his pillow half covering his face,
Trump whispers, "Nobody likes me in the Presidential race".*

"Why, Melania? How can this be?
I really love myself as everyone can see."

"So why does everyone look down upon me?
Could it be that I am too 'God like' and brilliant for
the bourgeoisie."

"Speaking of God, I launched a new Biden attack,
He is against God, don't you think that will set him back."

"By evoking God's wrath,
Lightning bolts will disrupt his campaign path."

"But Donald", Melania retorts,
What if God decides to strike you instead for sport."

"After all, haven't you been the one playing fast and loose,
With the Ten Commandments' holy truths."

"Don't worry Melania, I will skate free,
My fans are blind to anything shocking about me."

"Now roll over, go to sleep, but don't snore,
I am working on my role as the people's Coronavirus matador."

"The virus is like a raging bull pointing its horns,
It is what it is,* but I stand steady with stiff loins."

"Melania, this virus bull will soon die of old age,*
And I will be seen as the lion fresh from his cage."

"Donald, you buffoon, go to sleep, stop dreaming,
You are such an idiot to think what you do or say has any real
meaning."

* On July 31, 2020, with his poll numbers dropping, Trump complained that nobody likes him.

* On August 4, 2020, Trump said the Coronavirus "is what it is".

* On August 6, 2020, Trump stated Biden was against God.

* On numerous occasions Trump stated that the Coronavirus will simply go away.

by: Cora

INCREDIBLY, TRUMP ALLEGES DEMOCRATS WANT TO DO AWAY WITH COWS

A vote for Biden and Harris is a vote for no cows, *
With me there will be bovine flatus up to your eyebrows.

"Make America Fart Again" is my new slogan,
Democrats want to plug your cows' blowguns.

I say bring back the sweet smell of bovine gas,
Vote "NO" for any radical left jackass.

Imagine a world with no smell,
Of rotten eggs right out of their shell.

That's the world Biden and Harris will bring,
As their audacious vision is only fresh Irish Spring.

So, I say unto you voters with keen olfactory lobes,
I will keep bovine stench in your house and on the roads.

Vote for me, the King of crap's smell.
I will stop the Green New Deal's clean air hell.

---

*On August 13, 2020, Trump called the Fox Business Channel. He said amongst other outrageous things that Democrats Biden and Harris were against COWS. Presumably, he was lashing out against the «Green New Deal» that advocates for clean air.

RNC NATIONAL CONVENTION TO RE-ELECT
PRESIDENT TRUMP

Chairman Sean Hannity:

"The Republican National Convention will come to order,
We are gathered to re-elect our man Trump to heal our Nation's
disorder."

"We were planning a big crowd but then the Coronavirus hit,
So, we had to go virtual even though our flag bearer Trump
didn't give a shit."

"Now listen to Trump's trusted pals who are doing time,
Broadcast from their prison cells or home detention confines."

"It is a pity they couldn't be here today,
Sad victims of fake news served at the deep state's buffet."

"What do you say to the American people 'O Chosen One'
Trump?"
Trump: "I am the only one between you and the Democrat chaos
dump."

"I may be a misogynistic tweeting creep,
But you have to re-elect me, for if I lose your 401 K's will weep."

"Since when does Biden's character and honesty matter?
I have proven my whole life that lies make the best tasting
batter."

"This election will be the most crooked ever,
Unless 'mail in voting' is ended by me pulling the 'stop' "lever."

"I have worked so hard to form a great base behemoth,
Consisting of hate groups, conspiracy theorists, and religious
extremists."

"I am so proud of this coalition,
Wonderful people who love our Nation."

"My fellow Americans, I accept your nomination for President,
My re-election will give me a chance to stifle any dissent."

Chairman Hannity:

"To celebrate this great event listen to the chorus of vocal phenoms,
The talented voices of Choir QAnons*."

"Singing "How Great Thou Art Master Orange Man",
Accompanied by the torchlight brigade band of the Ku Klux Klan."

*Sean Hannity is a Fox News commentator who is an unflappable supporter of Trump.

*QAnon believes there is a worldwide cabal of Satan worshipping pedophiles who rule the world controlling everything including Hollywood and the media. But for Trump this Cabal would succeed in America. Trump has embraced the group saying "they like me".

TWO SUBURBAN WOMEN DISCUSS TRUMP'S ACCEPTANCE SPEECH

Scene: Under the hair dryers at a Beauty Salon, each wearing masks and socially distanced.

L1: I am really depressed.
L2: Why is that?
L1: I watched Trump's convention acceptance speech last night. He accused that lovely man Biden of being a Trojan Horse.
L2: Well that could be considered a compliment if he thought Biden could wear a horse Trojan.
L1: Land O Goshen, you mean those stretch thingies that men wear on their dickies?
L2: Yes (blushingly)
L2: (After pausing), What got me is Trump said Biden will make all our manufactured goods labeled "made in China". Don't Trump and Ivanka make their stuff in China? Ties, dresses etc?
L1: Why yes, that is true. I don't think even his underwear is red, white and blue.
L2: (Laughingly) My, how you do go on!
L1: Did you see Trump continually pumping his fists?
L2: Yes I did. Imagine if a Black man did that.
L1: Seems like Trump likes to pump up the crowd by imitating a Rocky-like move. Shameful because he is the least Rocky-like figure you could imagine. A bloated, wobbly-legged man who appears to be about to tip over at any moment.
L2: Trump did promise a vaccine by the end of the year or sooner to kill the Coronavirus. But I thought he already had a cure. He says he drinks bleach everyday.
L1: If that is true, I would like him to lick all the bowls of my toilets in my home after he does so. (Laughingly)
L2: I know your hair is just about dry and you have to go, but did you hear him refer to the "White" House several times. Even to the point of turning and looking at it. It was transparent that he was rejoicing in the fact he reclaimed the place for the "White" race.
L1: Yes, and that he claimed to have done more for Blacks except for Abraham Lincoln. Bold, and, at the same time stupid. Seems he has conveniently forgotten the Civil Rights Act and Voting Rights Act signed by President Johnson. The list goes on

and on of more done by past Presidents that affected Blacks than by Trump.

L2: Did you ever notice that Trump is like a shoe salesman telling you that the shoes you are trying on look great even though they hurt like hell?

L1: Even better, he says that the dictator of China likes Biden when he himself said Premier Xi Jinping and he "fell in love." Also, he said he and North Korea's Premier Kim Jong-un also fell in love. Seems as though he has a fetish for tyrannical leaders.

L2: I agree he has many forbidden loves. Well, I am cooked. Time to go but I must stop at the gun shop to pick up my husband's AK-47 rifle. He is convinced after listening to Trump that Blacks are going to live in our suburbs and take them over.*

L1: Nice talking to you. See you next week at the same time. Remember, don't tell your husband that I am Black and I live just around the corner from you.

---

*Trump referenced during his campaign that he is putting a stop to low income housing being developed in the suburbs. The implication being crime will follow caused by minorities in these developments. It was a clear message to attract suburban voters by stoking fear in them.

MAD HATTER'S TEA PARTY

There he sits with his tea party guests around him in a cluster,
Mad Hatter Trump's barks at them are filled with hateful bluster.

"All are welcome except immigrants,
My delicious tea cakes aren't for them as participants".

"They can set the table and clean up our mess,
But they are unholy to drink my tea in their ragged dress".

"My special guests are protesters against "virus" stay-at-home orders,*
They like me and are my loyal supporters."

They are freedom-loving good people,
Just like the Charleston Neo-Nazis were under God's Steeple.*

Trump blubbers on to his tea party guests,
"Only use your right hand as the left is a pest."

"The main course is prime Coronavirus beast,
I captured it earlier than other countries in the world for this feast."

MELANIA'S RNC CONVENTION SPEECH

Shhh! Here she comes, strutting down the White House garden colonnade,
Stern, a half smile, her coal eyes flashing with new eyeshade.

Undulating, a model-like stroll, moonlit,
While dressed in her designer gardening outfit. *

Gardener Melania spoke from the lectern in the late hours,
To an audience whose whiteness matched her newly planted flowers.

Using the replanted Rose Garden as a speaking forum,*
She used the occasion to show off her garden decorum.

She heaped praise on her husband's questionable record,
While omitting his predilection to stoke discord.

A briefing on her gardening activities would have been better received,
Rather than stretching the truth about what Donald has achieved.

To give her adoring audience sensual chills,
She could have demonstrated her tool handling skills.

Bemused by limited forced applause, she continued to stare,
Keeping an erect stance while swishing her Farah Fawcett hair.

Suddenly, Donald said, "honey the lights are being turned off",
It is time for us to go to our separate bedroom lofts".

"I've got tweets to send out while your speech is still germane,
Your awesome performance made Michelle look lame".

"At least this time you didn't plagiarize her words," *
"Alas, Melania, yours compared to hers are like moldy milk curds."

---

*Her outfit was criticized as having a military appearance but to this author it also had the look of fancy overalls that would be befitting a wealthy gardener.

*Melania totally changed the White House Rose Garden that contained vibrant colors of various roses replacing them with an all white array of roses.

*Melania's speech before the 2016 RNC CONVENTION was criticized for containing passages appearing to have been lifted from Michelle Obama's 2008 DNC Convention speech.

"It is my Garden and I will chew if I want to"
by: Gnelia

SUFFERING SUCCOTASH

'Tis me, your old pal Daffy Duck,
Sylvester, Bugs, Tweety, Porky and I are upset at Trump, the
dumb cluck.

He is a chicken whose self-proclaimed cleverness doesn't stick
like taffy,
Totally undeserving of my name, "Daffy".

People are insulting me when they call him "Daffy",
The world knows when an imposter is trying to be crafty.

From his squatting position he says things that sound crazy,
Come on now, you all know I am the bright one and not lazy.

His insane comments on Twitter and Fox News are like from a loon.
Suffering Succotash! Those statements wouldn't even get in
my cartoons:

1. Shooting a black man seven times in the back is,
   like a pro Golfer choking and missing a three foot putt. *
2. Biden is controlled by people in the dark shadows, *
3. A plane loaded with thugs dressed in black outfits traveled to
   the RNC National Convention. *
4. US soldiers who died for their country were "losers" and
   "suckers."*
5. Wounded Veterans shouldn't be in military parades. *

I mean, my "Black Duck Life Matters",
Call him what he is: a big looney chicken whose mind is in
tatters.

Oh no! Foghorn Leghorn, I didn't mean you, I was having fun,
Leghorn: (holding Daffy by his neck) Ah say, ah say, is that really
a joke son?

Sure, is Leghorn, I didn't mean any harm,
Just pointing out Trump is the odd man out on this farm.

As a matter of fact, Trump is imitating you again and again,
Saying, "I say what I say", when asked about disparaging
McCain.*

Whew, that was close! Didn't want Foghorn to twist my neck,
Should have said Trump was an addled old cowboy missing
cards in his deck.

Yikes, I did it again! Sorry Yosemite Sam, I am out of
here lickity split,
Yosemite: (Chasing Daffy) Come back here you Muley Headed
Maverick.

SOUNDS OF MUSKET FIRE: THAT'S ALL FOLKS!

---

*On August 31,2020 Trump said on the Laura Ingraham Fox News program that some
police officers "choke", like a pro golfer missing a three foot putt when referencing the
shooting of Jacob Blake who was shot seven times in the back in Kenosha, Wisconsin
by a police officer.

*In that same interview Trump claimed that Biden is controlled by people in the "dark
shadows" and made the unsubstantiated claim that a plane load of thugs travelled to
the RNC National Convention.

*On September 1, 2020, The Atlantic magazine published an article alleging that Trump
called deceased US soldiers "losers" and "suckers".

In that same article Trump said that wounded veterans shouldn't be in military parades
as it would make the public uneasy.

*On September 4, 2020, Trump said, "I say what I say", when asked about disparaging
the late Senator John McCain. He also said he was not a fan of McCain.

BAD, BAD DONALD

Come on man, confess,
Admit it, you scammed us.

You admitted downplaying the Coronavirus threat,*
To stop a panic in the US.

All the while knowing adults and children would die,
You decided to serve it up like warm apple pie.

Telling us that it was like a flu that will just go away,
Is just like saying a hurricane is just a wind so enjoy the sway.

Face it Donald you are a bold-faced liar,
Unfit to lead our country during this virus quagmire.

Telling the truth is not one of your traits,
You fine-tuned lying while a realtor snake.

Wake up Donald, get a clue,
As leader of the free world you are a Cuckoo.

I mean, really, even the Lone Ranger wore a mask,
Your reluctance to do so clearly shows you are not up to the
task.

Your gibberish on the campaign trail,
Is something to behold, like slime from a sickly snail.

Your curious habit of wearing hats with slogans,
Must give you the feeling of being a Hulk Hogan.

But face it Donald, you are the epitome of disgusting,
No Superhero, but similar to a feckless teenager having trouble
adjusting.

---

*On September 9, 2020 Bob Woodward released tapes wherein Trump admitted to
intentionally downplaying the severity of the Coronavirus. He claims he did so to calm
everyone.

SAY WHAT?

Trump says, he "saved Prince Salman's ass,"
Referring to the dismemberment of Khashoggi's entire body
mass.

Deferring and avoiding any criticism of the Prince,
Trump gave his Royal Highness time to give his bloodied hands
a rinse.

Rather than investigating Khashoggi's grotesque murder, he put
it aside,
Putting his dirty money hands over this country's moral pride.

He praised the Prince's purchase of American war machines,
While remaining silent about the assassins' handheld guillotine.

If that wasn't enough, Trump claims he deserves a third term,
He says the way he has been treated means a free pass to
return.*

It's becoming overwhelming, the distasteful words from his filthy
mouth,
His adoring fans must have filters that have gone south.

Saying Biden is "shot",
And that he doesn't know if he is alive or not.

Degrades the discourse voters should receive,
On such an important election's eve.

But if that is what he wants,
His opposition can toss equally potent taunts.

Such as "Hey there Mr. Prostitute man,
Been to the Sauna lately for your latest body slam?"

Or, "Your Ronald McDonald uniform needs cleaning,
You must have dribbled when doing your hair preening."

Or, "When you pump your fist and stumble across the stage,
You look like an overweight cheerleader not acting his age."

So Mr. Trump, aka "SUPERCON", go to your room,
Read that Bible you held up to see why to save even you, Jesus
rose up from his tomb.

* Trump made this statement to Bob Woodward. It is reported in Woodward's 2020 book entitled, "RAGE".

*On September 12, 2020 Trump claimed in a Nevada rally that he is entitled to a chance at a third term based on the way he has been treated.

HYPROCRITE OATH

Senate Majority Leader "Moscow" Mitch McConnell presides and speaks:

"Will the Republican Senators stand to take the Hypocrite Oath, Raise your right hand to swear to tell the truth, lie and do both."

"Repeat after me:"

Truth is one thing, lying another,
I pledge to mix them both together.

Whatever I said before,
It is my God-given right to ignore.

I will always flip-flop with persistence,
I have every right to be inconsistent.

Truth is whatever I say,
It is squishy and can be changed everyday.

It is not my fault that the public may get confused,
No worry, just pick one of my statements, you've got nothing to lose.

---

*Administered to Republican Senators after the untimely death (September 18, 2020) of Supreme Court Justice Ruth Bader Ginsburg after the question was raised as to whether her successor's nomination and confirmation process should be held after the impending November 2020 Presidential election and/or the swearing in of a new President. Many Republican Senators had previously stated when President Obama nominated Justice Garland after the death of Anthony Scalia in March of 2016 that the voters should decide in the Presidential election who should be the next Justice. Senate majority leader Mitch McConnell refused to advance Garland's nomination on that basis. Now with Justice Ginsburg's death he said the opposite. Clearly hypocritical.

IT IS ALWAYS SOMEONE ELSE'S FAULT

Don't open the Obamacare exchanges,
Let the uninsured pay virus bills with their own change.

Anything with Obama in its name,
Won't pass the mustard in my lane.

Obama left the virus cupboards bare,
What was I to do, just sit there and stare?

No, I had to reinvent the whole virus response,
From the ground up I created a virus renaissance.

So what if I delayed my preventative actions for you folks,
Initially, I said this Coronavirus was a Democrat hoax.

So my new line of attack and reason for delay,
Is to blame China for not telling us earlier of this viral doomsday.

After all, Obama pulled the wool over your eyes,
He was utterly incompetent to no one's surprise.*

---

* On May 17, 2020, Trump said President Obama was utterly incompetent.

DONALD, IT'S TIME TO LEAVE

Scene: At the front door of the White House after the November 3, 2020, Presidential Election

Knock Knock, Donald, are you in there?
It's Joe Biden, I need to move in my office chair.

Donald, where are you?*
Yoohoo! You lost to you know who.

So, show your face and come out here,
Stop hiding. We will find you and bring you out in the clear.

Be a man and face reality,
You are not wanted in this house any longer, so flee.

Come on now, don't sulk and cry,
Stand tall, grin and say bye, bye.

Rise up, show some dignity and pride,
Even if it hurts, pick up your stride.

But first you must come out of hiding,
Facing the music is part of surviving.

Maybe go to the kitchen for a snack,
Have your last succulent Big Mac.

With your stomach full and after wiping your drool,
You will realize you are acting like a crazy fool.

So pretty please, come out wherever you are,
Don't make this messy, just slink out and get in your car.

What's losing an election anyway?
In the scope of things you've got time to really make hay.

You can write about your foreign leader lovers,
The title could be ME AND DICTATORS UNDER COVERS.

Leading up to the November 3, 2020, Presidential election, Trump refused to commit to a peaceful transition of power if he were to lose to Biden.

"Drumph the Grouch"
by: Joey

TRUMP'S MESSAGE TO JOE

Ha, ha, Joe, you don't live in the White House,
I do, * you vacant-headed louse.

No way you'll keep up with my name calling,
I have years of practice resulting in my opponents falling.

I am casting you as an anti-law and order guy,*
I will shape you as a sissy and me a warrior riding high.

My caravans of flag-waving dupes will flood the city streets,
Parading my Trump force attack squads in the face of liberal elites.

Who cares if there is violence and protests of police brutality
My people are my tentacles acting as my instrumentalities.

I am sending more trucks carrying my supporters waving
American flags,
Choking off all Democrat inner city's main drags.

Next, I will send waves of humming evangelicals holding up
Bibles,
Chanting my name and disparaging my rivals.

Lastly, my golden image on a float decorated like one of my
hotels,
Pulled by a team of illegal immigrants fresh from their cells.

Can't stop me, Joe, even if you try,
The American people prefer a lying showman over a nice guy.

---

* During his acceptance speech at the RNC convention, given in front of the White House, Trump turned to the White House and said he lives in it, Biden doesn't.

*In late August 2020, Trump emphasized Law and Order as his main topic in his campaign resulting from violent protests due to several obvious incidents of police brutality. He put emphasis on the violence coming from cities controlled by Democrats.

WHITE HOUSE PERSONNEL HAVE STAR WARS LOOK

Scene: Two persons see White House Staff members in a bar
next to the White House

Wow! What a circus!
Strange creatures here. Sure they won't hurt us?

No, they are pretty weak, like a mouse,
From having survived the Covid-19 virus in the White House.

Unfortunately, they were left disfigured by virus mutations,
Comical in some respects but downright ugly creations.

Look in the corner, looks like something poured from a jar,
Yikes!, it is Attorney General William Barr!

All sticky and slimy like molasses,
The spitting image of Jabba the Hutt but with glasses.

Look! Over there, seated at a table with cards spread,
Appears to be a small silk worm with a minister's head.

Shh, it is Vice President Pence, now an Evangelical dealer,
Playing cards with his multiple feelers.

There are so many unique and interesting living things in here,
Long-nosed faces, spiny heads, scaly bodies, sagging ears.

There is an interesting one, a cross wearing fairy,
That, if you can believe, is Kayleigh McEnany, Press Secretary.

Yeah, the virus really twisted her around,
What used to be her front now is a backside with a frown.

There they are, look who is coming in,
It is President Trump and Melania with their trademark grins.

Melania, once a swan-like creature,
Now her long neck has blistered bubbly features.

She is wearing signs all over her body and glands, To hide the
fact she has stubby wings for hands.

As for her husband, President Trump, he indeed looks odd,
A Chewbacca-like thing definitely not created by God.

His hair, once prominent on his head, is now all over his body,
Wearing curlers to prevent looking shoddy.

Moaning his insulting speech, trying to be a heavy hitter,
His daily disgusting dribble continues on Twitter.

Yes, a sad looking group in this bar,
The lesson: the virus comes in when you leave the door ajar.

"Bill Barr at the Bar"
by: Gnelia

TRUMP'S STRANGE ENVIRONMENTAL VIEWS

" I know more about windmills than anyone,"
Trump spouts, "on this subject I will not be outdone."

"They kill birds, are noisy and give off fumes,
Look underneath, you'll see dead birds brought to their doom".

"I want clean air and pure water,
You see I am an environmentalist*, the world is not getting hotter"".

Forest fires raging in the West are not because of climate change,
They are caused by poor forest management across the range".*

"Climate change, what is that?
Probably a term made up by a radical left brat".

"Not even science knows what is causing horrific wildfires,*
The world will get better on it's own, who cares if it is drier"?

Melania: "Donald Dear, on the phone is a Park Ranger,
He wants to know how many fallen trees present a danger."

Trump: "I'll take the call and tell him the facts,
Clean up those trees or be fired for failure to act".

Ranger: "But hundreds are down, some at 6000 feet",
Trump: "Shush, if necessary, I will send troops with rakes to sweep."

Ranger: "How many trees do you want them to clean"?
Trump: "All of them, I want the forest to be like a putting green".

Ranger: "But fallen trees provide nutrients for new growth",
Trump: "Poppycock, dead trees cause the forest to go up in smoke".

---

*In August 2019, Trump claimed to be an environmentalist after skipping a group at the G-7 Summit that was focused on the Climate, Oceans and Biodiversity.

*In December 2019, Trump went on a rant about windmills causing environmental damage.

*Trump made this remark as historic forest fires were spreading across the Western US in September 2020. *On September 14, 2020, during a visit to California, ravaged by wildfires, Trump said, when confronted about the connection with climate change, that he didn't think even science knows.

THE DOMINATOR

Just like Arnold Schwarzenegger is the terminator,
I, Trump, am the Covid-19 virus dominator.*

My brush with this virus was a "blessing from God"*,
My medicines kicked those virus peas out of my bod.

Even though 100,000 previously died from the flu,
People lived with it, that should give us a clue.*

Live your lives, go about your ways,
Open up the States, don't become virus slaves.

While we do that, Bill Barr, my dear Attorney General lawyer,
Put Obama, Biden and Clinton in jail forever.*

---

*On October 6, 2020, Trump said don't let the Coronavirus dominate you and he said, just like the seasonal flu, you have to learn to live with the Coronavirus.

*On October 7, 2020, Trump demanded that Attorney General Barr put Obama. Biden and Clinton in jail.

TRUMP'S CRAZY TALK

So what if I re-tweeted that Osama Bin Laden wasn't dead,*
I enjoy spreading mischievous crap to get in your head.

I am the re-tweeting tycoon,
Here are some that I am sending very soon.

1. Jesus is not dead,
    He is a caddy at my Mar a Lago spread.

2. Hitler is not dead,
    He is Pelosi›s beautician going by the name «Ted».

3. Stalin is not dead,
    He, Putin and I often share the same bed.

4. Suharto is not dead,
    He is my butcher, serving prime beef and
    delicious bread.

These are just a few of my new re-tweets to come,
I think they are great, maybe not for some.

But you know, sitting as President can be a little boring,
So why not cause a little excitement rather than snoring.

So Poo, Poo Piddly Dew,
My re-tweeting endears me to my crazy fan crew.

---

*During Trump's Town Hall on October 15, 2020, he admitted re-tweeting that Osama
Bin Laden was not dead.

BYE, BYE

Scene: Trump confronted by a voter at one of his rallies:

Trump: "If I lose this election to miserable Joe,
I guess I will leave the country as fast as I can go." *

"It 's not that I want to leave but things will look bleak,
Losing to the worst candidate ever will make me look weak."

Voter: "Look here, Donald, your departure would be great,
At last the air waves won't be full of hate."

"So pack your bags and brush your teeth,
We will all wave goodbye and breathe a sigh of relief."

"The only thing that will greet you if you return,
Are warrants for your arrest that you can't spurn."

"So enjoy your junket across foreign lands,
In your absence we will be a community holding hands."

"As far as we are concerned you can take all your wigs,
And give them to your adoring lover dictator pigs."

---

*On October 17, 2020, at a rally, Trump said he might have to leave the country if he
loses to Joe Biden, as he is the worst candidate ever.

LOOK WHO'S TALKING

Trump called CNN "dumb bastards",*
For news coverage about the virus he claims he mastered.

Should we tolerate his vulgar words?,
Verbal missiles from his mouth are like rancid cottage cheese curds.

Yet, he goes on and on right in front of us,
Throwing noted Dr. Fauci under the bus.

Calling him and other scientists idiots,
Whose only sins are trying to protect us from a virus so hideous.

In the feverish days before the election, he has become unhinged,
Leading his fans way out on the fringe.

Curiously they remain in line,
Showing no independent thought or courageous spine.

Hup, two, three, four, they march to his wacky tunes,
Marching like sickos chasing a helium balloon.

It remains a mystery as to why and how this can be,
When his lies are so outrageous even a child can see.

I guess it really boils down to this,
Trump's politically dehydrated fans still drink his stinky piss.

---

*On October 19, 2020, Trump, at a rally, called CNN "dumb bastards" for continually covering the Covid-19 Pandemic

"Stinker"
by: Gina

YOU WANT YOUR KIDS BACK, TELL US WHERE YOU ARE!

Come out wherever you roam,
All 545 children we separated from you need to go home.*

So what if we have been unable to find you,
Your kids have been well fed, not like in a zoo.

OK, I get it, there has been some trauma,
Especially, at midnight, when little ones cry for their Mama.

We usually wear ear mufflers to muffle the noise,
They eventually cry to sleep surrounded by thrift store toys.

Some do experience night terrors,
But we strap them down and provide safety barriers.

I am sure you will agree child separation was a great plan,
Discouraging immigrant parents from coming to our USA land.

Putting up with whimpers and tears is part of the job,
The greater good demands we look past their sorrowful sobs.

---

*It was announced on October 21, 2020, that immigrant parents of 545 children could not be found after they were separated from their children and deported. Trump's plan was to deport parents separately from their children. It was a way, in his thinking, to discourage immigrants from coming in the first place.

ELECTION 2020 DERBY

Announcer: Welcome to the election issues derby,
We've got a fast track that's definitely not murky.

This special derby is run every election,
Horses are named after issues chosen by your selection.

However, two candidates are racing today: GoJoe and
SuperCon*.
The latter is a late entry because he withdrew his protest at
dawn.

SuperCon had claimed he should get a head start,
Saying he has the most magnificent horse in the park.

The horses are lining up and entering the starting gate,
The fans are crowding the rail and can't wait.

The horses are getting restless. There is the gun!
The mighty beasts pound their hoofs not to be outdone.

Would you look at that!
SuperCon and GoJoe are leading the pack.

Close behind are Covid-19 and Healthcare,
Both are sleek, fast sprinting mares.

Climate Change and Racial Injustice are hugging the rail,
With Economy Stupid and Foreign Relations nipping at their tails.

As they round the curve some dirty tricks are being played,
SuperCon is dropping libelous e-mails attempting a blockade.

He is up to his old tricks,
Seems he can't win a race without dirty politics.

The issue horses are catching up to these two fellas,
Pacing themselves so they don't become overzealous.

Now they are neck and neck with Covid-19 by a nose,
Wait a minute! GoJoe has added some speed to his toes.

He is beginning to pull away,
As the issue horses keep SuperCon at bay.

Economy Stupid and Foreign Relations fall to the rear,
Racial Injustice is now behind Healthcare who is in high gear.

Threatening to pass SuperCon is speedy Covid,
Holy cow, SuperCon is throwing mud.

SuperCon screams, "we are passed the Covid threat,"
"I have done nothing to regret."*

SuperCon violently strikes his nag with his whip,
Covid-19, alongside him now, bites at his hip.

Like shot from a gun, GoJoe pulls well into the lead,
Lengthening his stride atop his mighty steed.

Turning from his leading position,
GoJoe yells, "if I win do you agree to a peaceful transition?"

"No way in hell", barks SuperCon, "I will stay the course,
Riding my horse all the way to the Supreme Court."

"Screw you", says GoJoe, "I just passed the finish line,
I am in the winner's circle, you are an unpleasant memory in
time."

---

*GoJoe refers to Joe Biden and SuperCon to Donald Trump

*Trump repeatedly stated ad nauseum that the country has rounded the bend as to
recovery from the Covid-19 virus while actually at the time infections were on the rise.
When asked if he would have done things differently concerning the virus, he replied
"not much". That statement was made in the face of over 225,000 Americans having
died from the virus at that time.

ELECTION EVE AT THE WHITE HOUSE

Melania: Now, Dear, drink your bleach like a good boy, put aside your insults,
You need to rest so you will enjoy this evening's election results.

Trump: "Did you wear a mask and gloves when you mixed this brew?,
Even though in public I don't do either, I want you to."

"Melania, tell me again how great I am,
My fans tell me so all across the land."

Even so, I am behind in the polls,
Maybe this pandemic is taking its toll.

"You know, I never read "Laudato Si",*
The book the Pope gave to me."

"Maybe God is taking revenge on me for our planet I ignored,
I may regret withdrawing from the PARIS ACCORD."

"Perhaps my marital affairs and profane mouth,
Pissed off the man/woman upstairs enough to lose all my clout."

"Dammit! Melania you are a woman, last time I looked under your blouse,
Ok, OK, I know it has been a long time since we played house."

"But, tell me, why don't suburban women like me?
After all, I am the greatest at everything, wouldn't you agree?"

"Take your time to respond, but it is hurting
my presidential quest,
I hope your answer won't make my ego regress."

Melania: "if you really need to know what they think,
You are a sexist bully, not fit for the garbage disposer under their sinks."

Trump: Well, that is not good news,
I hope you don't share their views.

Melania: Don't worry, Donald, it is our little secret,
I told those blondes you don't use the disposer, so don't put that in the leaflets.

---

*Encyclical by Pope Francis with the subtitle, "On Care Of Our Common Home" in which he warns of environmental degradation and global warming.

WHAT ME WORRY?

Having Covid-19 is no big deal,
My Proud Boys pals and I pretend it is not real.

I didn't want to go to the hospital,
But I was coaxed to do so after everyone was afraid of my
spittle.

So I faked some symptoms just to pretend,
A fever was detected by a thermometer in my rear end.

To me, my little cough and chills were no concern,
I am a tough guy whereas a wimp would have heartburn.

So after being cooped up in the hospital for a couple of days,
I took a little joyride in my armored SUV to give my fans a wave.*

But, I forgot a Bible to hold up to the glass,
To show I am the chosen one to conquer this Covid-19 task.

To heck with others being exposed,
I am the only important person, as everyone knows.

Some might call me selfish, an egomaniac troll,
But with my royalty wave I showed the world that I am in control.

After four days of hospital care,
I bolted out like a newborn hare.

So what if I was flushed in the face,
I felt twenty years younger ready to get back in the presidential
race.

Maybe a little woozy and stiff as a board,
But can't let the virus dominate my spinal cord.

I got on my helicopter for my next performance,
Flying to the White House to give my Oscar winning entrance.

From my balcony I stood with my skin slightly aflame,
Silently posing majestically having beaten the virus dragon lame.

I ripped off my mask to the cheers of the virtual crowd,
Like a Conquistador who just stuck his lethal shroud.

I gave a stern thumbs up with dramatic flare,
Signaling my hospital enema had worked with no room to spare.

While visibly breathing heavily, I saluted the empty space,
Like the Statue of Liberty, I was the sentinel of grace.

Sean Hannity said I was like FDR or Churchill,
Slaying the virus dragon with very few pills.

I am the greatest warrior of all time, man,
Even while squatting and panting on my oversized bedpan.

---

*On October 1, 2020, Trump tweeted that he and Melania had been diagnosed positive for the Covid-19 virus.

*On October 4, 2020, Trump was widely criticized for taking a joyride around Walter Reed Hospital in his large SUV to wave at fans while he remained an inpatient.

ELECTION EVE PRAYER

Now I lay me down to sleep,
I pray tomorrow we don't re-elect that creep.

I wish I may, I wish I might,
Wake up tomorrow free of election fright.

I will snooze away until sunrise,
Hoping to rejoice in Trump's election demise.

Trump pledges to hand the election off to his lawyers,
After the votes are counted, to be election destroyers.

Then, to add to the absurd, he said he is going to fire Dr. Fauci,
Rounding up this trusted Covid-19 doctor with his Trump posse.*

I hope these thoughts don't keep me awake,
Maybe, I will just stay up and bake a big chocolate cake.

---

*On November 2, 2020, responding to chants at his rally to fire Dr. Fauci Trump stated he would take that up after the election. Dr. Fauci is a highly respected virologist who has served as an advisor to both Democrat and Republican Presidents.

BULL FROG

A large Bull Frog sits on his White House Lily pad,
Looking over the Washington DC swamp, feeling so glad.

There are so many potential, disgusting fans out there,
That his long venomous tongue can pull into his lair.

He speaks with repeated croaks,
Trying to incite fears amongst American folks.

These croaks are loud and full-throated,
Making him sound larger than he is, even when fully bloated.

He patrols the Lincoln Memorial Reflecting Pool,
Hopping and dipping to keep his slimy skin cool.

His tiny front legs flap feverishly when he speaks to his crowds,
Hunkering his bullhead like an emperor between bows.

Curling his webbed front leg fingers to make a fist,
He pumps them wildly while attempting to throw a kiss.

When interviewed he squats in a forward-leaning position,
Waiting impatiently to throw a false zinger proposition.

To prevent the interviewer from getting the upper hand,
He emits outrageous conspiracy theories from his stinky glands.

Leaping from one lily pad rally to another,
He stops momentarily to croak incoherent bluster.

When croaking he blows up his jowls,
Mumbling words seemingly coming from his bowels.

Seeing him play golf is a howl,
Riding in his golf cart smothered in cold wet towels.

His small fingers stroking his putter while waiting his turn,
He repeatedly croaks, "no one will ever see my tax returns."

He sees himself as a frog that can never do wrong,
That is why he sits lonely in his White House pond.

He only thinks of himself, making up stuff that is pure baloney,
Being an outcast within his Republican colony.

Most frogs make adorable pets,
Not this one, however, he is a psychological mess.

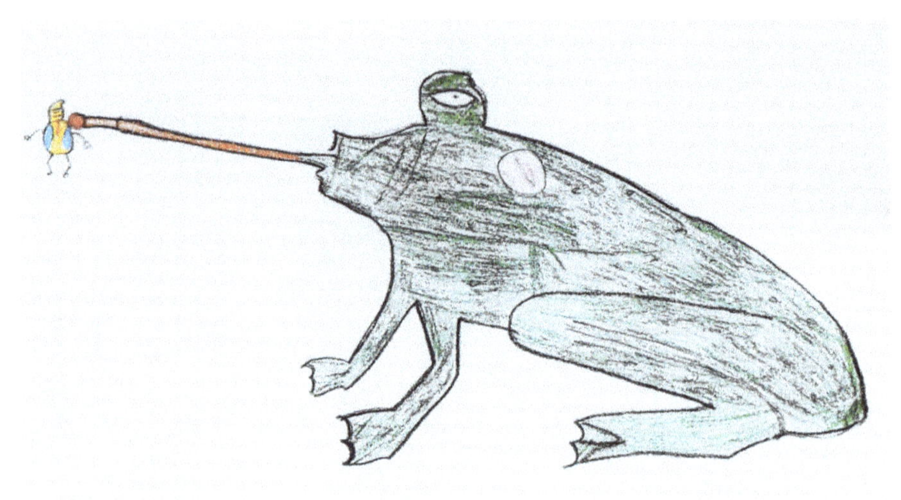

"Bull Frog"
by: Walker

WITH TRUMP AFTER THE POLLS CLOSED

Tweeting from his cuckoo's nest,
Trump issued erratic ramblings to create civil unrest.

He complained illegal ballots were mounting,
Saying he would only lose if late votes were put in the counting.

Relying on his infamous whines,
He circled himself with crooked allies picked from his poisonous vines.

How could he lose to Sleepy Joe? What a bunch of crap!
What would he do with his large inventory of red hats?

Oh no, the final news came in,
The race was called for Joe Biden.

What should he do, Trump whispered to himself?
Should he let his hair go natural and put orange dye on the shelf?

After all, he doesn't care about the country's good,
He only cares about protecting his questionable manhood.

So he began preparing for his new TV starring role,
Swimming with alligators and conquering sci-fi trolls.

He may be too blubbery for a Tarzan suit,
But his Sumo body will shine in the "Adventures of the Spandex Brute".

A TALE OF TWO STATES
TRUMP LOSES!!
FIXED!
FRAUD!
FAKE!
PHONEY!
SUPER!
SPECIAL!
SUCCESS!
FLORIDA
CALIFORNIA

by: AI

TRUMP'S POST ELECTION SHOWER SONGS

Show me the way to go home,
I am drunk with power and need to go to bed.

Had a little election about a month ago,
And it went right straight to my head.

Wherever I may roam,
On land or sea or foam,
Show me the way to my sweet Mar a Lago home.

Kumbaya my Lord, kumbaya,
Kumbaya my Lord, kumbaya,
Kumbaya my Lord, kumbaya,
Oh Lord, kumbaya.

I am not crying my Lord, kumbaya,
I am not crying my Lord, kumbaya,
I am not crying my Lord, kumbaya,
Oh Lord, kumbaya.

I won big my Lord, kumbaya,
I won big my Lord, kumbaya,
I won big my Lord kumbaya.
Oh Lord, kumbaya.

Send in the troops my Lord, kumbaya,
Send in the troops my Lord, kumbaya,
Send in the troops my Lord, kumbaya,
Oh Lord, kumbaya.*

Throw the Bidens out my Lord, kumbaya,
Throw the Bidens out my Lord, kumbaya,
Throw the Bidens out my Lord, kumbaya,
Oh Lord, kumbaya.

Make me the winner my Lord, kumbaya,
Make me the winner my Lord, kumbaya,
Make me the winner my Lord, kumbaya,
Oh Lord, kumbaya.

I am your chosen one my Lord, kumbaya,
I am your chosen one my Lord, kumbaya,
I am your chosen one my Lord, kumbaya,
Oh Lord, kumbaya.

Melania, we tried it once or twice,
We found it rather nice.

Roll me over, lay me down and we'll do it again,
Roll me over in the clover, lay me down and we'll do it again.

Don't forget the White House monogrammed towels,
To lay on in the clover to protect my weak old bowels.

---

*Trump and his advisors discussed the possibility of declaring martial law in certain swing States and sending in troops to redo the election in those States.

THE QUEUE

We are all in the Queue,
Yes, even me and you,

Standing shoulder to shoulder,
In a line that includes the younger and older.

Waiting for better days to come,
Looking forward to getting rid of the Trump family scum.

A rainbow arc begins at the Queue's gate,
Extending beyond out of sight as we start a new slate.

But before we can proceed to the new day,
We have to endure Trump's nonsensical asinine bray.

Acting like a stubborn mule hee-hawing frivolous lawsuits ever
so frail,
He refuses to move off the election trail.

Fearing that he will be called a loser or a flop,
The gears in Trump's mind have ground to a stop.

His political supporters refuse to take his reins,
To pull him away from stopping the inevitable Queue train.

Despite his attempts at election insurrection fame,
His post-election conduct will be an historical asterisk marking
ignominious shame.

But sooner or later he will move his carcass,
Being remembered only as our Presidential catharsis.

OH, PARDON ME!

Trump gave pardons to two birds, one a Thanksgiving Turkey,
The other, Michael Flynn, the jailbird jerky.

The Turkey was a big fowl festooned with beautiful colors.
The other wore a gray, black-striped uniform like all his felonious
brothers.

How many others would escape the Prosecutorial quest,
And fly from their prisons' nests?

Turns out the Turkey and Flynn were just the start of the Pardon
Parade,
Pardons to insiders and war criminals made the process
a smelly charade. *

Trump led the Parade thumping his Pardon Mace,
To the tune of BORN FREE while sometimes goose stepping in
place.

The pardon recipients hummed along,
Snickering, laughing and breaking into song.

They carried photos of their prosecutors and sentencing judges,
With their images blurred with irreverent smudges.

What made it a truly festive event,
Was seeing gleeful Trump family members huddled under the
pardon tent.

Singing and dancing filled the evening air,
Fox's Hannity, Ingraham, and "the Judge" slouched in their
chairs. *

A fantasy election bar served voter fraud cocktails,
Under the sponsorship of the estate of the late Roger Ailes. *

As the bartender's "last call" was bellowed,
Stumbling pardoned guests all burst into a Trump salute, "FOR
HE'S A JOLLY GOOD FELLOW.

While waddling about, Trump bumped into porn Queen Stormy Daniels,
"Oh, Pardon Me", he said like a sullen Cocker Spaniel.

"Your wish is granted", Queen Stormy proclaimed,
"Now, your place or mine to resume our titillating games?"

---

*Trump pardoned political cronies, convicted felons, and war criminals. The latter drew sharp international criticism, as they, employees of Blackwater, were responsible for a mass murder in Iraq.

*These three Fox News commentators remain committed champions of Trump's Voter Fraud campaign to overturn the 2020 Presidential election in favor of Trump.

*Roger Ailes was the former Chairman and CEO of Fox News who died in 2017. He left Fox News under the cloud of sexual harassment.

YOU ARE FIRED! THE PEOPLE HAVE SPOKEN

Hello Donald, have a seat. You are fired!
Four years ago you were mistakenly hired.

Your annual reviews have been miserable,
Nothing short of abysmal.

Donald, how could you lie every day,
And think that we would want you to stay.

Yes, we heard it all in your self-gloating tweets,
About how you were the greatest President to ever walk the streets.

But your promises don't match your performance,
You spent more time golfing and pursuing Dictator romance.

You made it easy for us. You don't fit in our vision,
Especially with your plans to squat in place contesting our decision.

What is with you anyway? Trouble at home or brain inflammation?
Whatever it is, we can't give you a good recommendation.

So, clean out your desk and sneak out to save face.
We've chosen a real President named JOE to take your place.

Please, Donald, we know you are upset about us showing you the door,
But don't do your usual and pee on the floor.

THE GOP SENATE NURSERY

Here we are in the Senate playpen,
The Red Hats are like babies. Led by drooling Mitch, their
mother hen.

Look there, baby Rubio dropped his rattle,
Mitch hid it and told baby Cruz not to tattle.

Meanwhile the baby Red Hats,
Began a loud screaming spat.

Shouting, "the election was a fraud. It is illegal to keep us
penned up,
Supervised by Democrat socialist nuts."

Thrashing and spitting, the Red Hats threw a tantrum,
Causing beagle-eyed Mitch heartburn.

"I will not clean up your protesting mess", he exclaimed,
"How does my GOP put up with you? Have you no shame?"

"Just because you disagree with the rest of us,
Doesn't give you red hats the right to raise such a fuss?"

"Even most adult babies are cuddly and sweet,
You Red Hats are ornery, so I will strap you in your extra large
car seats."

INVASION OF THE RED HATS

Sparked by inflammatory words,
The Red Hats marched into the Nation's Capitol undeterred.*

Pushing and shoving, they charged through its doors,
Desecrating its sanctity, parading its hallowed floors.

Carrying a Confederate Flag and hanging a noose,
These thugs broke windows and destroyed property while on the loose.

Trump's words having branded violence into the Red Hatters' brains,
They marched hypnotically as if insane.

Under Trump's rhetorical spell, the Red Hatters screamed and shouted,
While their cowardly leader sulked and pouted.

During his flaming speech urging the crowd to insurrect.
Trump promised he would meet the Red Hatters on the capitol steps.

Like all cowards in history, however, Trump words were hyperbole,
He watched the Red Hat insurrection lounging in front of his TV.

Content to watch the rebellion from afar,
Trump didn't call reinforcements to quell this nation's new seeping scar.

He tepidly said, "Just go home," and like mellow tea from a kettle,
Gave soothing words, I "love you" and "you are very special".

It was ever so predictable that he would go down in flames,
But a mystery as to why regular folks would join him in ruining their names.

---

*On January 6, 2021, following a speech laced with vitriol, President Trump directed his large crowd to march on the Capitol to disrupt the Congressional vote certifying the election in favor of Joe Biden. The crowd developed into a mob and caused property damage and loss of life after breaking into the Capitol.

THE END OF TWEEDLE INSANITY

Four years couldn't go by fast enough for some,
But Tweedletweet (Trump) and Tweedledum (Pence) sure had
fun.

Tweedletweet's lies that sprinkled his bumbling tweets,
Were voraciously gobbled up by Neo-Nazis, extremists, and his
Red Hat fleet.

Tweetledumb sang identitcal twin Tweedletweet songs,
Playing the dumb pal so he could deny conspiring all along.

Their odious ride in office came to a screeching halt,
When the 2020 voters decided to lay them in the ex-president
vault,

Puffing up like blowfish to strike at their prey,
They began spewing unverified charges of foul play.

Thinking and saying they won the 2020 election hands down,
Both Tweedles summoned the Red Hats to town.

They were convinced they had won by a lot,
Only lost because of leftist fraud plots..

But surprise! Tweedledum voted to declare Biden the winner,
In response, the Red Hats chanted "hang him" with our noose
stringer.

The Red Hat mobsters yelled "death" for Pelosi and Schumer,
Ventilating once again their sadistic brain tumors.

By a mighty push and rush,
Thousands of Red Hats stormed the Capitol in a despicable
gush.

Fearful, Tweetdledum sought shelter from his Senate dais,
Meanwhile, Tweedletweet enjoyed watching the Red Hat riot.

Lounging in front of his TV, Big Mac in hand,
Tweedletweet sat in glory watching the Red Hat marauding band.

Patriots! He exclaimed, expressing love for them,
Like a nurturing mother watching them play in their playpen.

Enjoying the chaos created from the Red Hats suckling on his tweets,
Tweedletweet sat on his hands thinking this is so sweet.

Tweedledum, to save his own skin, looked in a new direction
Separating from his twin, Tweedletweet, who caused a treasonous insurrection.

Will Tweetdledum be an honest stand-up man,
Or just an imitation made out of Spam?

As for Tweedletweet, he will sit by the roadside,
Selling MAGA paraphernalia still convinced he won by a landslide.

History will eventually reveal the impact of the Tweedles' Presidency,
Many already thinking it was a four-year asylum residency.

No offense is intended towards that great novel, "Through The Looking Glass" by Lewis Carroll in which Tweedledee and Tweedledum were delightful odd characters.

GET ME OUT OF THIS BURG ADDRESS

President Lincoln gave a magnificent Gettysburg address,
Trump on the other hand couldn't get his election loss off his
chest..

Still complaining as he turned off the lights,
Yelling, "doesn't anyone see my plight?"

"The demon socialists defrauded me of my Presidential nest,
Can't everyone see that of all the Presidents I was the best?"

"I nurtured peace in the world by loving our enemies,
So what if they sting us like sea anemones".

"As for the climate, burn, baby, burn,
Light the coal fires, make the pollution cauldron churn".

"I fulfilled my promises to re-light fossil fuels,
Fanning the environmentalist vs. miners duel."

"My fans will always remain in my saddle bags,
While I ride as their champion, never raising the white flag."

"Me surrender, absolutely not!
Even on my last day, I stood defiant like their Lancelot."

"On my cue, my people cried USA, USA,
So charming, calling for me to slay their prey."

"Only thing they don't know is I am a chicken that leads from the
rear,
"Go forth! Press my cause against socialist smears."

"The Gettysburg address called for unification and healing,
My "Get me out of this burg" address was to leave before my
staff began squealing."

HE'S GONE

Bye, bye, Trump to you and your clan,
Thankfully your ilk was a flash in the pan.

No tears are shed,
We all look forward to a good night's sleep in bed.

You did teach us one thing though,
Lies, deceit, and self-gloating only belong in sideshows.

When the damage you have done to our nation becomes clear,
Pause for a moment before primping and preening in the mirror.

Look down at your bloated McDonalds belly,
Think how your Presidency could have been great instead of
smelly.

Take your golf clubs and see if you can even get a partner,
No one wants to play with a recalcitrant kindergartner.

At least now, when you slip into your paranoid delusions,
It is all on you and not on our precious union.

So enjoy yourself surrounded by your Foxie pride,
With Mucker Carlson, Hyena Hannity, and Snarly Ingraham at
your side.

All of you can sit around telling favorite delusional stories,
As the world goes ahead, searching for its future glory.

TRUMP'S WORDS MATTER

Impetigo makes one itch,
Having poison ivy is a bitch.

Surviving four years of Trump is a test of stamina,
Like recovering from a bite from a poisonous Tarantula.

Scratching can provide temporary relief,
But it won't cure the bite of Trump's words, not even brief.

No use trying topical ointments on your body and head,
Won't work trying to dream them away in bed.

They linger in your thoughts,
Like the horrible sound of grasshoppers eating your crops.

What is so sad is, while the salve of truth can heal,
The deniers relish his words eating their skin's peel.

WHAT WOULD PAUL REVERE SAY

One if by land, two if by sea,
Look out your window and you will see,

The Red Hats are coming!
Swarming like lemmings.

Their QAnon* flag flies,
While their Orange-headed leader chants lies.

They are carrying nets to catch their prey,
Searching for pedophiles they say are not visible in the day.

The Red Hats claim legislators are part of a subversive group,
Wanting Trump removed from Congress's coop.

No one will be safe, so hide your children and wife,
The Red Hats show no mercy with anyone's life.

We must be clever to thwart their advance,
By showing their stupid ignorance.

We will dress decoys in pedophile costumes,
Our troops will wear face masks of Fox News hosts from
its newsroom.

After blending in, the QAnon troops will be destroyed,
By our fake "insider" Fox hosts as they viciously attack the
decoys.

If we catch one or two and question them,
We may learn who their leader is, causing this mayhem.

As of now, we think we know his/her identity,
It goes further up than our Trump clown obscenity.

If Congresswoman Marjorie Taylor Greene* is a person we can
trust,
She says the leader is made of cosmic dust that floats in at dusk.

---

*A conspiracy theory alleging that a secret cabal of Satan-worshipping, cannibalistic pedophiles is running a global child sex-trafficking ring and plotting against Donald Trump, who has been fighting the cabal.

*Congresswoman Marjorie Taylor Greene has made numerous outlandish statements in her life. At one time she suggested that the California wildfires were caused by a Laser beam from outer space at the hands of the Rothchild family and PG and E.

THE NEW GOP

Given how gullible the new GOP is to conspiracy theories,
Here are somo that demand their serious inquiries;

Elephants can fly,
Elvis is alive,
Hoffa survived,

Jesus's image was seen on Trump's golf bag,
Jews play outer space laser tag,
A pedophile cabal has taken over our press rags.

These can be added to the conspiracies spread by the GOP,
In all their glory for everyone to see.

All of the idiotic Republican theories are to be engraved in stone,
At a GOP holy site where non-believers can atone.

Trump, being the father of the new GOP,
Will have his name in bold letters over an arched canopy.

There will be a statue of him larger than any of our founding
fathers,
Behind Greek pillars set on either side of an extravagant altar.

Picnickers will spread out their blankets full of treats,
Surrounding the Trump holy place mumbling his tweets.

QAnon will have a concession stand,
Selling on parchment their conspiracy theory brands,

Of course Ivanka will hawk her women's wear,
Wearing nothing but a sandwich board causing a stare.

Like a Cuckoo jumping from its clock, Trump will appear,
Standing on top of the monument pumping his fists to his fans'
cheers.

As the sun sets on his tangerine face,
He will retreat back to Mar a Lago to continue his life of disgrace.

GOP SENATOR LAMENT

It's not that the evidence didn't prove Trump should be impeached,
It is just that I don't want him to be impeached.

I am supposed to sit as an unbiased Juror,
But this is politics so I don't want voter furor.

I realize that history will show I was a dipshit,
But my only option with my constituents is to acquit.

Yes it will be hard for me to explain to my wife and kids,
However, if I convict, Trump will come after us with his slanderous pigs.

You know who they are,
They are the Fox News snarly stars.

Anything non-Trump is greeted with disdain,
No matter if it is the truth they will twist into a lie without any strain.

Pompous and self-gloating,
They side with Trump in his self-promoting.

So, you see what I am up against in Fox land,
Unfortunately, my people only turn their dial to that band.

Maybe my way out is for me to vote with a bag over my head,
That is decorated with a Democrat face instead.

I know it is hard for reasonable people to swallow,
But we Republicans are bonded to Trump with whom to wallow.

To break that bond will require some guts,
The question is how do I do it without being called a putz.

BOZO, YOU SAW THE NOOSE

Standing ready for Pence's neck was a hangman's scaffold,
Finely built, big and bold.

A newly woven noose dangled from a beam,
Prepared for a lynching spawned in the mobsters' dreams.

Clearly visible to an approving President Trump,
Who was watching the insurrection in a slump.

Not appalled, he sat enjoying the mob's offense,
Turning his eyes away from the noose meant for Pence.

By not looking, he was trying to preserve his denial,
That he did anything to warrant his impeachment trial.

He lounged before his big TV snacking on munchies,
While the police were overrun and injured by his Trumpies.

To him, the violence and hate on display was a grand sight,
Feeling proud that his hateful speech contributed to the fight.

Let's see if he promises to pay the insurrectionists' legal fees,
Like he has in the past when violence occurred at his rallies.

VIOLENT CLOSURE

The end of Trump's four years,
Brought our proud nation to tears.

A violent insurrection that destroyed property and lives,
Was the result of electing a man who doesn't even cry.

As the nation wept,
Trump peacefully slept.

At peace with himself, not having any concerns,
Of the carnage, person killed, or lives overturned.

Still triumphant, he sat, a recluse,
As the wind swayed Pence's noose.

You would think such a thing would bring
The GOP into the impeachment ring.

But no, the GOP with few exceptions sat on their hands,
As the Donald Trump impeachment trial began.

The expected unfortunately came true,
The GOP blocked his conviction on cue.

The tearful Nation watched Mitch McConnell explain his vote to
acquit,
Eloquently, he gave reasons to convict but then made our
heads split.

Saying that there was no jurisdiction to try this fool,
Caused even Lady Justice to drool.

That position had already been overruled despite a GOP lobby,
But yet, beady-eyed Mitch ignored the Senate body.

Mitch claims to be a man who follows the rules,
But it is clear in this instance, he was played like a fool.

However, he was praised for his conviction analysis reflections,
He left no doubt of Trump's guilt for causing the insurrection.

As expected, Trump recoiled against McConnell's jabs,
He accused Mitch of just about everything, except having crabs.

Lack of wisdom, skill, personality, political insight were on the list,
Along with dour, sullen, and political hack. Wow, was he pissed!

It is again intermission in the life of Super Con Don,*
But his acts of retaliation, sniping, and stupidity will go on and on.

The lingering question our GOP friends will have to deduce,
Would they even have convicted Trump if Pence's head dangled from that noose?

Having lost the election after serving only one term and being impeached twice, Trump took up residence at Mar a Lago to plan his political future and defenses against many outstanding lawsuits.

THE REAL CONSPIRACY STORY

On March 4, 2021, Trump is to take over the USA,
At least that's what QAnon says.

This conspiracy plan has grown,
So Trump can get back on his throne.

However, the real story is that Trump laid eggs,
In the White House kitchen's flour kegs.

If we had looked closely, Trump's rotund profile,
Wasn't just a sign of his high carb lifestyle.

In actuality his swollen belly was from visitors from outer space,
You see, Aliens impregnated him while he adored their cute
faces.

Thinking he had just eaten too many Big Macs,
He paid no attention to his growing embryo sac.

He laid his eggs just before he left the White House,
Not even telling Melania, his spouse.

So instead of Trump returning on March 4th,
Alien babies will hatch and lead the discourse,

To prove this is not a cockeyed view,
We knew if Trump lost, there would be a visit from an alien crew.

Congresswoman Greene spilled the beans,
By saying Aliens were sending us laser beams.

What she forgot to say,
Is that these creatures were also coming here to stay.

What more perfect vessel could there be,
For them to fertilize an unsuspecting Commander in Chief.

After the alien babies emerge from their hatch,
They will immediately begin wearing red hats.

Later, having been trained by QAnon loons,
They will tweet outlandish conspiracy cartoons.

Thus, continuing to twist vacant minds,
Leaving reality far behind.

PLAY BALL

Here it is, opening day.
On the mound is Moscow Mitch to pitch the first play,

He is known for his curveball pitch,
But he throws a mean slider, driving batters into the ditch.

You just can't trust him as to what he will throw,
Batters that did, ended up in the dugout's first row.

His spit ball is really gross,
With sticky chunks of his morning toast.

He splitter is something to behold,
Going every which way, so I am told.

With his forked tongue flashing and his pitching arm flexed,
No one can guess what he will say or do next.

He tells his manager one thing he wants heard,
Then he tells his dwindling fans something else absurd.

Take, for example, his criticism of the Trump insurrection mob,
He turned right around and said he would endorse that nut job.

His pitching style reflects his scrambled brain waves,
Making him unable to follow the signs his catcher has made.

His goofiest pitch of all,
Is his crazy screwball.

It hops and jumps as it approaches the batter's box,
Confusing even the catcher out of his socks.

The GOP fans chime in, giving their fastball "heater" chant,
A pitch that he throws after rubbing it on his pants.

Trying to oblige and stay in good stead,
Old Mitch is easily confused and combines his pitches instead.

With the result that he is not sure what pitch is which,
Causing his fans to finally scream "ditch the Mitch".

GOP's GOLDEN MESSIAH STATUE

A golden statue of Trump had C-Pac fans in a trance,
Despite being gaudy, it was greeted with reverence.

Dressed in American flag attire,
His pose was that of a religious GOP Friar.

With the US Constitution and a magic wand in his hand,
He looked like a sorcerer come to save our land.

He wore Jesus flip-flop sandals,
To portray his closeness to heavenly angels.

His flag-striped swim shorts did seem to sag,
While covering his loins with the American Flag.

His large head looked as if in a daze,
About the same as a Hippo, half crazed.

What was intended, no one knows,
But this golden idol was the hit of the show.

The C-Pac crowd, in its anxiety to be bold,
Created a profane monster in glistening gold.

---

*At the Conservatice Political Action Conference (C-Pac) held in February 2021, a
golden statue of former President Trump was unveiled.